Travelling
Alphabet
Emotionally

The story
of a life
full of lessons
as lived

By

Sylvia Clare

Also by the same author

Raising the Successful Child,

Trusting your Intuition

Living the Life You Want – with David Hughes

Releasing Your Child's Potential

Heaven Sent Parents – with Kelly McKain

The Well Mannered Penis

The Musician Muse - a book of Poetry

Thanks to David Hughes for the Cover art work, the Fruits of Life, and all the love, support and encouragement anyone could ever ask for. He is my one true soulmate.

Published by Clarity Books 2018.

Introduction

The cliché of life being a journey is only a cliché because it is so true. We are all on a living trajectory which takes us towards many places internally and externally, geographically and emotionally too. This is the first book in the series 'Travelling the Alphabet' – a collection of stand-alone essays and observations on my experiences of various dimensions of life.

The title was born from a game I made for myself, some thirty years ago or more, which was to travel to at least one country of every letter of the alphabet. Politics and age may prevent me from completing that goal geographically speaking but through visiting such diverse places I realised that my travelling had brought about another kind of journey, into the inner woman.

Sometimes I can hardly remember the younger me, this girl who miraculously grew into an adult woman and yet sometimes she comes back so clearly that it is like yesterday, and I realise that the memory was less the issue than realising how far I had come in those decades.

Collectively these essays tell my story, not because I think my story alone is especially important but because I learned a great deal from it and would like the opportunity to share that.

You can read the sections in order, but they are all stand alone essays and can be read by dipping in and out just as easily.

Even as I wrote the originals and now edit them for this first collection, I can see how much I am still changing daily. So when this is published, I will already be in a position to update it all again, or not!

I feel as if I am finally coming of age, that I am becoming who I always felt I was on the inside but could not express. Finally, I am fulfilling my young teen intuition that I would somehow become a writer, never an ambition but just a quiet knowing.

I owe so much to those whose paths I have shared, for better or for worse, and I have been as kind as I can be to them all, although the best experiences from which to learn are not the most pleasant to live through.

But I especially owe a huge debt of gratitude to my husband David, who has helped me along so much of this journey and whom you will meet in these pages often. He also does my soundtracks and artwork as a gifted creative in his own right. He is the light of my life, my most treasured Dharma sharing Sangha of two, my mentor and my love.

I am equally grateful to my two sons who have been wonderful teachers of so many of these lessons and I have also inflicted these lessons upon them in their own lives, for better or for worse. We have all come through it together, loving each other in spite of tough times.

One never knows the outcomes of one's own efforts in life, but I hope more than anything that those reading this can find something that is useful to them within its pages and that my journey can light the passageway for others too. What more can anyone want in life?

Essential acronyms

ADHD – Attention Deficit Dyperactivity Disorder
ADD -   Attention Deficit Disorder
ASD -   Autistic Spectrum Disorder
PTSD -   Post Traumatic Stress Disorder
NPD -   Narcissistic Personality Disorder

Index

Understanding Emotional Complexity 6

A is for Acceptance 10, Altruism 15, Anger, Anxiety, and Abuse 18.

B is for Bereavement 28, Bliss 33, Boundaries 46.

C is for Change 56, Compassion 64.

D is for Depression 71

E is for Equality 76, Expectations 81.

F is for Food 87, Forgiveness 94, Friendship 107

G is for Gratitude 112

H is for Honesty 118, Humility 127

I is for Intuition 136

J is for Jealous and Envy 147, Joy and happiness 151,

K is for Kindness 154

L is for Letting go 160, Love 164.

M is for Money 173.

N is for Narcissism 178.

O is for Orgasm   187.

P is for Past 198, Peacefulness 201, Praise and Criticism 203,

Prejudgments and Prejudice 206.

Q is for Questioning 212

R is for Relationships 215, Responsibility 222.

S is for Self-Acceptance 224, Shame and Guilt 227, Silence 233.

T is for Time 236, Triggering 238, Trust 245.

U is for Uncertainty and all the Uns 250.

V is for Victimhood 252, Violence 254.

W is for Worrying 259, and Wrongness 261,

XYZ is for Extras and Zany stuff 270

Last Word 273

Understanding emotional complexity

Before I get into individual emotions, and the lessons I learned about them, all from experience and practice as well as extensive reading and study, it is vital to understand the following if we are all going to become more emotionally literate. Emotions do not happen in isolation and they do not happen individually. They are very complex human experiences which we can sometimes be completely unaware of in ourselves, and sometimes can be completely taken over by also, and to our own detriment.

Layers of Emotion & Understanding Happiness

We tend to think we are all just experiencing one emotion at a time.

We are not.

Emotions layer up on each other.

We can feel many things at one given time, but we may only be aware of the surge of whichever is the dominant emotion at one time.

We are not taught to explore all or even be aware of all those layers, yet they can be so informative for the journey into self knowledge and self awareness.

Mindfulness practices vary slightly from one tradition to another. But in most of them, mindfulness of emotional and physical states is very important, crucial even to this whole journey into mindful ways of living.

If you stop right now and focus for a moment, take a deep breath and then clear your mind of extraneous thoughts.

What are you feeling right now?

Travelling the Alphabet Emotionally

I could give you a list, I am hungry because I mostly only eat twice a day and I am nearing my second meal time. I do count off the last three hours or so until I start preparing that meal lol. But I do not view hunger as a problem state to experience. For some people hunger is associated with loss of love, anxiety and all sorts of other states and emotions. Craving food is easy to overcome once you recognise these additional emotional attachments to them.

So what else am I feeling right now. A slight sense of adrenaline as I am writing this piece, concentration and reflection going hand in hand with furious fingers trying to keep up with my thoughts.

But along side that I am also quietly celebrating, my temporary but wonderful pain free state for now. I saw an acupuncturist this morning for pain relief for my arthritic spine. Although I view pain like hunger, just a sensation to be explored and experienced, I am happy to be free of it for as long as this lasts. Apparently, I (my body at least) responds very well to the needles.

I can hear my husband moving around doing all sorts of home improvements upstairs and I feel a sense of deep calm knowing he is doing that, gratitude for all he does to make our home wonderful. I also feel huge amounts of love for him just for existing. In the same way I can feel that kind of love for my sons and grandson, just by thinking of them in their own homes. So if asked 'how do you feel', superficially I could say one thing, but if I stop and consider I can identify many different emotional states all running simultaneously, not competing with each other, just each doing their own thing.

Travelling the Alphabet Emotionally

We have a wonderful tradition in the Community of Interbeing—followers of Thich Nhat Hanh. We ask each other how our internal weather is. This allows for more complexity that just 'fine thanks' can ever express.

We might say 'blue skies and sunny but some clouds gathering in the distance'—or we might say—'storms cloud passing over head but patches of sunshine coming through'. We might just say 'wall to wall gloom' or 'blanket sunshine' but rarely is that the case. The nuance of weather reflects the nuance of how we actually feel at any given moment. It allows us to be more honest without details.

I can add to my list above that I have deep sadness ongoing for a young member of my family who is deeply unwell. I can also say that I have, underpinning all these other emotional states, a foundation layer of deep and enduring happiness which often shines through me even without me knowing, but other people comment on it sometimes, usually to my husband. I glow somehow. That is truly based on deep love for everyone and all things.

Perhaps it is my aura or my energy field, or my chakras, who knows. I don't mind which explanation is used. All I know is that I do indeed have this huge well of happiness. And even though, every so often, my old darkest habit energies come back to remind me of where I have travelled from, I can usually even then, touch through to happiness and if not experience it, just know it is still there slightly and know it is simply waiting for me to return from what I loosely call the hell realm based on Buddhist terminology. We have multi layers of emotion but probably just two main ones, on the surface which responds to everyday stuff and the one underneath. Can you identify where these are for you, or how these are for you?

Travelling the Alphabet Emotionally

My underneath constant used to be terror, throughout my childhood, with superficial attempts to pretend otherwise, and to avoid any more grief from my parents whose presence felt like a constant threat.

But I changed that deeper layer to happiness through a lot of hard work and mindfulness practices, healing the damage done by my unmindful and damaged parents. I believe how we teach children to show and experience emotion is utterly crucial for the long-term welfare and mental health, especially the terrible divides between genders, which I have explored in more detail in my books 'The Well Mannered Penis', and 'Releasing Your Child's Potential'.

I still, and probably always will have, all the surface emotions in response to the daily ups and downs, shit and stuff, like everybody does. I am simply human like everybody is.

I know deep down I am amazingly happy and at peace with my life but not dishonest about how hard some days still get to be, or that I still get caught out by old habit energies which overtake me from time to time. Once you connect with both / all levels of emotional state, it is easier to manage them all xxxxx.

Acceptance

This word sums up a key developmental stage in almost all the positive, emotionally fulfilling mind states. It took me decades to reach it, and even now I can slip into frustration by wanting things to be different. Acceptance is the ultimate key to inner peace and contentment, to positive relationships

Acceptance is a process of 'allowing' instead of 'fighting with' what is.

I mean who doesn't want to fight all the things in life that are just plain wrong (in one's own eyes at least). We want to rage and rant at the world to justify our own position, our own paradigm, our own politics or ideology. We want to be right, most of all we want this! I certainly did and sometimes still do – when my ego takes control – until I recognise what I am doing.

We want to be right *and* we want to be happy.

We mostly socialise with like minded people who will affirm our rightness back to us. We seek that assurance from the media we choose to follow. We don't like contradictions to our world view and yet the world is totally chock full of them. And some of them have legitimacy too. Very frustrating – so we rant a little louder to try and drown out those dissenters to our world view. Or we refuse to speak/ listen to them. I have done this to people and I have had it done to me. We all tend to do this at one time or another and call it disagreement or incompatibility. But really it is our lack of acceptance of other perspectives.

Most of the racism sexism classism disability-ism and gender-isms stem from this lack of acceptance of 'other'. They don't think like us, so we become defensive and insecure and our response to that is to dominate and control to make it feel safe.

But that approach doesn't make us feel safe, and never will, because we cannot control anything in the universe for any length of time except ourselves. My parents tried to control me and they couldn't; I tried to control my children and I couldn't either. I tried to control my natural expression of myself to appease my parents and others who disapproved, but to do so was, and is, violence to self and I couldn't achieve it. I have the kind of personality that will out itself whenever it chooses and there is not a lot I can do about it. It is called having ADHD, and it is both a gift and a curse – but I have had to accept that this is how I am.

In the end we have to relinquish control.

Control doesn't work long term. Instead of trying to achieve peace or happiness through power and control, we must find it elsewhere.

Power and control

Acceptance says 'no, you cannot have happiness and control', instead you have to learn to accept differences. Life is full of opposites, dialectics even, (believing or accepting two things that appear to be direct contradictions / opposites of each other) that might just lead you to a better or more accurate perspective / answer. Look closer, go deeper, explore alternatives and open up.

What do we do to develop acceptance? Well it takes effort – when I look back, I have had a lot to accept in my life:

- like parents who did not want me or like me and told me.
- like my own total lack of self belief which I also defensively and ferociously protected and hid from everyone
- like I had finally found and married the most amazing man for me who would teach me that none of this was true and allow me space to heal.

That final gift took a lot of accepting because it went against everything I had been taught from early childhood. I am nearly there on that one, but my traumatised emotional system still needs regular reminding. He is endlessly patient with me.

I had a lot of accepting to do, one way or another, but to accept that everything you previously thought might be mistaken is huge, I mean it is really huge.

Just consider for a moment that everything you know is mistaken. How does that make you feel? Do you instantly hear those voices coming into your mind going 'but I am right about this or that or the other thing'? Do you now feel defensive or have you immediately gone back to 'no I am right about this – I am a good person'.

We place so much personal value and self respect on our belief system, on what we believe to be true about how things ought to be- but what if that were all wrong? That takes effort to even contemplate, let alone fully embrace.

I learned that adversity is how we grow most effectively, by finding our bottom line, by finding we can survive when we thought we might not be able to. Adversity is not desirable; we all wish to alleviate suffering – at least in ourselves if not in others. But some of my best emotional and spiritual growth spurts have come through adversity, and, through these instances of challenge, I learned acceptance.

Acceptance should be about 'how all things are' because everything is constantly in the birthing process of something else which might be very positive, but we might not be able to perceive this from our limited viewpoint.

Acceptance gives you calm and inner peace, it gives you serenity, it gives you an overview of life that transcends the daily ups and downs and allows you to make peace with what is.

Acceptance is a form of surrender to whatever life sends you – to what unfolds for you and those around you – and doing so with humility and grace.

Acceptance means noticing when you start to take a moral high ground about something, when you start to proclaim your victimhood, when you start to tense when someone says something that challenges your world view of 'HOW THINGS OUGHT TO BE', according to you!

Acceptance does not mean passivity or inaction. You can still stand up for things that you think are wrong in life, (injustices, inequalities, wanton destructiveness) and work hard to make the world a better place for the majority, if not for all. You can be a passionate crusader for the rights of those who cannot defend themselves.

BUT .... you cannot control the outcomes, thank goodness. If you think about it – that is too much responsibility for any one person, though some people are deluded into thinking they do have that amount of power, especially politically, and they may do in the short term, but that cannot ever last.

 Acceptance needs to be explored in this context to keep you sane, but still allow you to keep fighting the good fight for the greater good as you see it. After years of fighting this campaign, or that issue though, I have come to realise that much of it is now so complex that it is hard to unravel without having an unintentional adverse consequence elsewhere, which was not part of your intended plan.

All you can do is to accept your part in creating all these injustices in the world merely by being part of it, the interconnectedness of everything which none of us can escape and do what you can not to collude or enable them to continue.

You can accept your potential to undo these same injustices, by changing behaviours that contribute to it.

Sometimes without you even realising it, but now you can accept that responsibility and make that change and then just accept that others will take time but eventually things will change as they inevitably do – always and without fail.

Accept that you can do your little bit, you can be part of the solution and stop being part of the problem, but you alone cannot do more than that. Acceptance is huge and it is part of all the other dimensions of emotional journeying that I hope to take you on in future articles. It is worthy of our deepest consideration.

Altruism

Being kind to others, with no obvious benefit to yourself. Is it such a hard thing to do?

Altruistic behaviour is what in Buddhism we call the behaviour of a Bodhisattva. This is someone who has practiced their meditation sufficiently to dissolve most of the Ego or self and thus can act accordingly without any self-interest. Zen master Thich Nhat Hanh suggests we never lose our entire ego because it is also our will to live and in part why we develop our practice in the first place – to be happy.

I have heard arguments or discussions where people say that altruism doesn't really exist because it cannot be done for 'someone else only'; you benefit in some way, by feeling good about yourself for having done a favour.

Is that always true though? And does that matter? Are we not entitled to value ourselves and have good sense of self for being the best version of who we are? Of course there are do-gooders out there who want everyone to know how 'good' and 'kind' they are so that they can use this to boost their self esteem.

But is this wrong?

Unless there is a 'deal' of some kind then I would argue not. But if there is a payoff involved, then there is some kind of control/manipulation going on which can lead to unhealthy dependency behaviour patterns setting in. You can disable someone by doing too much for them. You can take away the reciprocal nature of friendship by giving too much. You can try to buy indebtedness by over-imposing your kindness. And none of this is altruism. Altruism cannot really be assessed by yourself since you cannot see how you behave as clearly as others might.

We really are so very good at deluding ourselves that we have no agendas of our own when we often do.

Nowadays having worked on reducing my sense of self, I can notice that I don't really have a reaction to helping others other than an impetus to do it. A friend is dying and I just feel enormous compassion for her suffering in those last stages but I don't feel a need to do anything for myself. I do feel an automatic response to her suffering to do what I am able to do for her, what she wants me to do and what is practical for both of us. I don't think about what I want to do or not do, I just see a need and do my best to fulfil it.'I' do not appear to be in that equation and 'I' am relieved by this. It is like everything I do. I see something to do and my body does it or doesn't do it but there is no reaction either way. I can also see how different this was from before I experienced an enlightening moment (more of that later) when I can see that 'I' was always in the equation, I always wanted to help, to be helpful, and now that isn't something that occurs to me, I just do it or not.

Is that altruism?

Since my enlightening moment of experience there is no fixed or constant 'me', I cannot be kind or unkind, it is up to the recipient to decide; it is their experience of me that counts for them, not who I am.

If we do something for someone else when we know there is a direct and unpleasant cost for our self, put our self in the firing line to protect someone else, take the flack to end the suffering of another, who is it that does that, the self or just an instinctive response? What really matters and counts as altruism? I know as a child growing up, I felt a very strong 'need' to protect both my younger siblings from the worst our parents could inflict. In some ways I did that at my own expense.

I took the flack for being the eldest and thus responsible for their bad behaviour by default, in my parents' eyes that is.

When we grew up and I really needed my siblings to support me and they stepped back and said no thanks, can't do that, I felt desperately betrayed and abandoned. It was some decades later that this happened, but I realised when it did, that they had embraced the 'it's all her fault' messages they'd been fed from childhood about me, but almost certainly, because of their conditioning, they would refute that even to this day.

But was I wrong to hope in my desperation that they would return that childhood favour? Yes! Because that meant what I did for them as a child expected a reciprocal and that was my mistake, too young to understand of course but that was still my mistake. If you do something for someone else, you must give it away - agenda free.

Well funnily enough although it mashed my sibling relationships into pulp, I think they were right. Without anybody knowing what the outcome would be, in retrospect I can see clearly that without their complete rejection of me during my breakdown I would not have gone so low and thus not gone into that moment of enlightenment which I have subsequently called 'the Lagoon'.

So their unkindness, if I want to label it thus, was a far greater kindness than I can ever repay. This is an excellent example of something I mentioned in acceptance about not knowing longer term and ultimate outcomes, and that they are often more positive than we expected.

What I am saying is that kindness is not always niceness. Altruism might be disguised in many forms and quite unintentionally. Nothing is as it seems superficially, but on a day to day basis I want to live with kindness and non –judgement, gently and openly, there is no better way to live, from experience, and I have lived through a few.

Embrace all experiences as potentially positive and see how that affects you emotionally.

Anger, Anxiety, and Abuse.

These are dauntingly huge topics and have been massive parts of the challenges in my life , but here goes!

Superficially these three items appear to manifest quite differently, but my experiences of them are all commonly rooted in fear and thus can be explored collectively. Whilst I believe that many more people have been subjected to abuse than will recognise it, we can all identify with experiences of both sides of anger and anxiety, through projecting it onto others, or being on the receiving end of it.

Finally, I justify this lumping together of such nasties by suggesting that without anger and anxiety, abuse might not exist in quite as many and diverse ways as it currently does, on both familial and socio/political levels. Who hasn't felt the heat of anger or the gnawing sensation of anxiety in their life and probably more frequently than anyone would like, or even admit to? They can be invasive emotional states to experience, overwhelming at times and yet not utterly unnecessary. After all both anger and anxiety are parts of our early warning system, so we need to explore and understand them fully to be able to manage them.

This takes courage and determination but is preferable to the alternatives, expression or suppression, both potentially very destructive. But this is what most people unconsciously do with these tricky emotional states, which then cause far greater harms further on.

We often suppress anger and fear because of social discrimination as a result of expressing any challenging and strong emotions. We fear reprisals and rejection for our openness of these emotions and are never given any solid guidance of how to manage or deal with them constructively.

It is the lack of understanding of anger and anxiety that leads to its more abusive expression. This creates a mounting problem that spills out in self-destructive behaviours that hurt others. I have personal experience of all angles of this emotion, having been on the receiving end, and also dishing it out.

I shall start with being on the receiving end. In my early years I was subjected to a terrifying level of anger from both my parents. My mother, as the eldest of three sisters, projected her inner self-hatred onto me, as the eldest of her three children, - she literally hated me in private - and then proceeded to take her anger with herself out on me, her three, four, five, ... yr old child, for some misdemeanour, when I never quite understood what I had done wrong. I got blamed for upsetting her, whereas in reality the anger that foamed and frothed out of her came from within her. All that I may or may not have ever done as a child was to trigger it. She had no skills with which to even recognise or manage this trait in herself other than denial.

That is never the fault of any child; you, me or any other child on the planet. Children are just children. They do what children do. They are never or rarely intentionally nasty or cruel to others except in innocence due to lack of the developed skills of compassion and empathy and often that is due to the lack of positive examples being set with those qualities by the adults around them. There really is no such thing as a bad child – sure difficult ones – ones who struggle themselves – but the adults around them are there to manage this not to create mental illness in future adults by their abusive mis-treatment and anger. Yet this is the lot of so many and thus their challenge to learn to overcome – in their own lives.

It took me years to stop being angry with my mother for the anger she threw my way.

But in the end I realised this gave me a double hurt and once I let it all go and realised how unhappy she had really been, I felt more compassion for her than anything. She was in the end more terrified of me than I was of her. Denial and accusing me of lying were her only defense to her dying day. When I told her I had a publishing contract to write books on emotionally intelligent parenting, her only words to me were 'don't expose me, will you'.

I never did explicitly while she was alive and I only write about her now with kindness and compassion but also honesty about what a hellish life she had, of her own making by holding onto all the anger that her own childhood generated in her. My father's anger arose out of my mother's emotional abuse of him and making it impossible for him to 'get it right'. She was a classic narcissist, a 'hungry ghost' wanting something external to help her feel loved, and valued, and all the other conditions we need to feel in order to flourish and be our best selves. It is an impossible demand to place on another person and my father was emotionally ill-equipped to begin to know how to cope with her needs. As her first child, the expectation was transferred to me and then I too could never 'get it right' with her.

His anger took two forms. The first was his overuse of smacking which turned into him using me as a punch bag for venting his anger with mum and the world. His anger was also about being expected to 'do something', 'to be *the man*', all far more distressing and unkind than the quiet life he yearned for. The second was his icy cold withdrawal of all love or kindness from me. His eyes could kill me again and again.

Like many, he didn't understand that the quiet life comes from within, so he got angry with anything that threatened that quiet life from outside instead.

They had the same problems in many ways, which is why they brought out the very worst in each other, that impeccably accurate mirror which shows us who we each are if we know how to look into it. If you look into the mirror of life and you see anger then don't blame the mirror, but if you don't understand that principle then you will blame the mirror, and this will set up a reverberation between you and the mirror, which simply increases all the time, until something like anger becomes ultimately destructive. The same is true in the opposite form of course. If you set up love and gentleness in your mirror, then this will increase all the time too. Most people have a rough balance of these two emotional forms and their variations but this balance between the inner and outer is another step to understanding happiness.

The other form of his anger, which in many ways was far more terrifying, was the withholding of his love. He did that with his eyes, which would turn cold steely, empty and full of contempt, looking down on me with hatred at my existence. Those were the single most terrifying times in my life. In those times he did not see me as a human, as anything that had any value - he would probably kill if he thought he could get away with it, to remove the cause of all this strife.

That is where I think my earliest PTSD trauma came from, that and the constant barrage of anger from my mother.

That is what my inner child reacted to when I saw him again, just before he died and caused me such a deeply traumatic reaction, which was both the best and worst thing in my whole life. A breakdown that lasted six years and taught me so much, that enabled me to write this book.

Anger is a destructive energy if it is not understood properly but can be a very positive energy when dealt with intelligently. I was very angry for years with both my parents for their lack of parenting and emotional literacy skills.

I was angry with my siblings for not sticking up for me when it really mattered, as I had stuck-up for them so many times over the years.

I was angry at other family members for not helping me or listening to me when I tried to tell them what was happening to me, for telling my parents what I had said and getting me into worse trouble.

I was angry with my teachers at school for taking sides with my parents against me and giving them more ammunition with which to reject me and pour scorn over me after every parents evening. Instead they could have helped me to find some way of connecting with the point of school, of overcoming the endless boringness of every moment in school in so many lessons. They could have encouraged my enquiring mind and curiosity, but instead wanted me to be a regurgitating sponge for information that just didn't grab my attention or appear to have any value in my life as I understood it at that time. That was my ADHD.

I was angry with myself for not being what my parents wanted and thus for failing in everything no matter how hard I tried, so that I stopped trying and allowed failure to take precedence.

I was angry with my body for not being all the things my mother told me it should be instead of how it was, too thin, too tall, too long, too big, too lanky, too piggy-eyed.

I was angry with life for forcing me to experience its ghastly misery of daily endurance, limping from one abusive experience to another, surviving as best as I could in between bouts of anger.

But I was also angry with society for its injustices, its cruelties, its famines and political failures, its cruelty of ideology and inequalities, its judgements and petty superficial values, its' authoritarian, punitive uncaring hostile attitude to those who fought back, said no, protested, wanted to be different or spoke out of turn. There had been so much anger poured into me in my life, and I was full of it in turn.

Growing up in the very repressed 50's and developing into adolescence during the 1960's meant that I could recognise the changes that were coming but I was not quite old enough or confident enough to be part of that – I could only watch and be angry that I was not old enough either. I wanted to race ahead into independence and break free, never to need family or anyone ever again. I was angry that I had no ability to trust anyone or anything, especially my own abilities or qualities. I was angry that I was desperate for someone to appreciate and validate me, a friend or partner, but none of them did.

It took me a while to understand that I had taken over all the abuse roles that my parents, teachers and society had started out with, that I didn't need anyone else, I could abuse myself. I did that, when what I really needed to do was to accept and love and appreciate myself instead.

Oh and to stop being angry!

That last part took time and came in stages but I found that if I turned my anger into action then it felt better, and I could stop being angry and just get on with doing something about it. Social injustice anger became positive righteous anger and made me engage politically, mostly feminism, human rights, and environmental issues but also injustice and related topics got me fired up to protest-march and sign petitions too.

I didn't like anger but I didn't know how to stop being angry about, and with, myself and others.

I suspect that is what many angry people feel like, so they suppress it. The trouble is this becomes pressurized and thus erupts every so often, when someone triggers that anger. And this is what happened with me.

I wanted to be the deep thinking, carefree, happy person I felt inside. I tried to present that external perspective to the world but inside the anger lay like a dark poisonous blanket I was permanently entangled with and smothered by.

I constantly fought to breathe through it, to find the light and air I needed to thrive. Sometimes people would trigger anger in me, just as I triggered it from my mother and father and gradually I realised I was just like them in some ways. That made me even more angry with myself!

When I wasn't angry, I was anxious, waiting for something to happen that terrified me and made me defensively angry all over again. A vicious cycle if ever there was one.

I tried to suppress anger ever more fiercely; it erupted more and more fiercely in response. Sometimes it came out on my own sons and I hated myself even more for that. I had been so determined not to carry the abuse through to another generation, but of course we always do, until we consciously let go of that same pattern of behaviour. Until we cleanse ourselves from its energy, it is now as much a part of us as anything else is. We didn't ask for it to be put there but we are now responsible for removing it. The emotional equivalent of fly-tipping, it can be a very costly business.

Anger evolves into other emotions too, like revenge and cruelty. I think my mother was cruel because she had no other way of expressing her sense of anger and shock at what had been done to her. I know I wanted her to experience what she was doing to me and thus we became more and more afraid of each other.

Revenge is defensive, it is trying to put things right from the outside, trying to make someone else stop by doing the same thing back to them. It rarely if ever works because it acts as an escalator of anger instead of an ameliorater.

Revenge starts out defensive and attempting to stop others but becomes its own cause as a release valve of what we are bottling up. We have to release the valve somehow, and others become the target, just as we were the target for the initial transference of anger and fear-based emotions.

The only way to end these cycles is to just stop in your tracks and work on the anger from inside yourself.

I know we are all still healing from it, me and my sons, as I write this, but at least I did stop it in myself in the end and then turned around to give them a hand up too. Additionally, we grow closer as family through that healing process, so good comes from struggle as always. I haven't ended my days perpetuating the abuse and anger and fear as my poor mother did, or running and hiding from it as my father did.

In the end I stopped being angry because it was so destructive for me, and once I had let all the suppressed rage and suffering out, there was no point in re-creating it any more. My skillfulness as a mindfulness practitioner by that time had grown to a level of self-awareness that allowed me to flow more openly with emotional states, rather than get stuck in them.

I still wasn't aware of the suffocating blanket weed of toxicity lying underneath everything in me. Trauma can haunt the body the same way it haunts memories; not only does the body remember a traumatic experience, but it can actually get stuck in the trauma response mode (PTSD).

Even when the immediate threat is gone, the body still perceives danger and its defenses stay on alert.

What is now generally understood, and biologically identified, is that when someone lives with that level of fear as a child, their immature nervous system develops exceptional sensitivity to any sign of stress or threat or danger and conversely is under developed in the neurology of happiness and sense of security.

They/ we become hyper vigilant for any signs or signals that echo what they have been terrorised with, which can make people hypersensitive,

Travelling the Alphabet Emotionally

In my case, I was emotionally frozen as a way of coping with that acute sensitivity. I still have to cope with that response too but can recognise and understand it in myself.

At a very early age, around three or four, I developed the ability to emotionally freeze myself so that I could cope with parental anger and my own anxiety. That 'skill', alongside their anger and abuse, created a deep layer of PTSD that lay inside for five decades, until my father's death caused the membranes holding it all inside to completely rupture. It was the only single event on the planet that would cause that membrane to rupture and it has been my salvation after the longest struggle not to be destroyed by it.

So anger, abuse and anxiety for me at least are very much woven into each other and are all part of each other. I am lucky I came out the other side and I am glad of the journey, glad for what I learned from it, glad for how it taught me not to use anger, glad for the joy I now experience every day, now that I have completed the journey through anger. I learned that anger, and anxiety, and abuse, are all scary monsters we hide from because we fear, believe, and think, they are valid judgments of us and who we are. If instead we pull them out into the light, name them as damaged children, recognise why they are there and hold them in compassion rather than judgment, then we can release them, bit by bit, until our life is free from them and their damaging influences and toxicity. I still allow myself some righteous anger though, I will still sign petitions and go on marches if I think it is important and it will bring about positive changes for others.

Any other forms of anger, as soon as I recognise it I dismantle it and dismiss it and inform it, it is of no value or use to me. Anything to disempower it and starve it of the oxygen it needs to grow again. What I want is to continue loving everyone and everything.

I can't do that if I allow anger to creep back into my life.

Developing skill sets in mindfulness and compassion have been my greatest gifts, my tools of choice, my ultimate healing weapon, the source of my deepest joy and happiness. The wonderful thing about mindfulness and compassion is that they too have the power of influencing neuro-plasticity and rewiring the brain into a happier and less vigilant mode. Healing does and will occur once you let defenses down sufficiently. No-one needs to stay angry or anxious; anybody can find happiness if they are prepared to work for it, if only my parents had understood that, but then if they had I might not be where I am now and that is exactly where I want to be.

I thank them deeply for their unhappiness in order to teach me deep joy and happiness, their sacrifice in life was my gain. It was a helluva journey though. I think they did both know happiness in some form later on after they parted company, and that makes me happy.

Bereavement

The older you get the more bereavement you experience. It is a fact of life – we are born, we live for a while, and then we die, and there is stuff in between that is called living.

This middle part – the actual living - is the point, but the confusion about life and death means that often we do not live, we are too afraid of the end to enjoy the middle part and thus miss out on it all.

Bereavement means a loss to you of someone or something on a permanent basis, but it does not often mean 'out of sight, out of mind'. In fact, it is the 'not out of mind' that causes us the most grief from bereavement. I lost three babies –two to early miscarriage and one to ectopic pregnancy, but I have two adult sons who are more than enough. Should I grieve for those I lost? I felt them. I knew them in a way as pregnant mothers do, even very early on. What part in my life had they played though?

At the point of writing this in the past few months we have lost three good friends, all to various forms of cancer and all far too young in our opinion since they were our contemporaries. They were all special but very different, all great losses, spaces left empty in our lives, but time moves on always and spaces do get filled eventually, in synchronistic and serendipitous ways.

'Hey, you are too young to die yet' - really means 'I am too young to die yet'.

I am officially an orphan too, both parents having died some years ago now. Their departure was a relief for me, liberation of sorts, the ending of an omnipresent sense of fear in life.

I cannot imagine what it must feel like to lose a much-loved parent. I cannot imagine that kind of loss in life, if it has been a good relationship.

Perhaps in early childhood I knew the sense of abandonment that bereavement brings anyway though?

I have also been bereaved of pets which have either got too sick or too old or too mad to live any more. I have cried deeply for them too.

Bereavement in every single one of these cases felt different. None of them prepared you for the next one.

There is a point in Star Wars when Obi stops – he has sensed a shift in the force – a mass departure, the extermination of a whole planet, and all who lived on it, by the death star.

That is how each death felt to me, a shift in the energy field of life around me, a momentary gap where someone once was, in whatever form. Some were harder to cope with than others. Some brought relief – an end to suffering – theirs or mine! Some took far longer to get over. There are three possible deaths I hope I never have to face, my two sons and my soul mate and husband, but I well may have to face at least one of them. I spent over a decade expecting to face one of the others though; it wears you down, hollows you out, so you slowly cut yourself loose emotionally, preparing for that moment. I believe that is a common reaction. Our fear of loss cutting us off from the life that is. That threat is now passed thankfully and I am free to love openly once more. We both missed out on a few years of good loving relationship though.

When my very close friend died last year, I was intimately involved with her end; to the last breath I sat with her day and night. I had wanted her to go, she suffered to the end, but when she told me she had been given the news that her cancer had reached the end stage and it was now down to days, I felt my heart leap out of me and I cried out suddenly in shock.

'We both knew this was coming', she said to me.

'Yes but not quite yet', I replied.

A day or so later I again found myself letting a sob out and saying I was going to miss her so much.

'I'm not leaving you, you daft bugger,' she said, in that fantastic Lancashire accent of hers.

I knew she meant spiritually, and we did agree that if she could she would come back and let me know what came next but I'm still waiting. I've been up to her grave a few times for a brief chat, but I know she isn't there anymore.

I just wasn't ready to lose her friendship and it had been a true friendship, a fierce loyalty to each other and a deep acceptance of each other's damaged histories and fight for a happy life. But she had lost hers and although I had so much and have so much in my life I still found the space she left harder to fill than I had imagined, until I realised that it never would fill in, it just wouldn't seem so vast once the rest of life filled in all the gaps around the edges a bit more.

You cannot replace people – but you do move on with what comes next and for me that was a second huge bereavement of leaving a house and more importantly a garden I totally loved. I know that year I was traumatised once more by the whole process of so much loss and change in one go, the intensity of it all nearly took me down once more.

My other most notable bereavement to date was non-human and deeply, profoundly spiritual.

I had a cat called Saffy who was also my power animal and spirit animal guide. She died fifteen years ago or more, but I can still remember that day so clearly. It was after lunch and she was suddenly and unusually climbing all over me demanding affection. But I pushed her off because I had to go and get more work done in the garden.

 I worked happily for about half an hour.

Then I was being called back to the front gate by my husband who was standing next to a neighbour and some strangers, all of whom looked incredibly anxious.

And there on the side of the road was my dead Saffy, run over by a jeep that was going far too fast up our narrow little single-track lane. She had jumped out of the hedge and run in front of the car without it being able to stop in time.

That moment everything froze, all I could do was to rush to gather her limp body into my arms and howl and howl with anguish. It was my first experience of real grief flowing through me like a river, energy in motion - emotional responses as they are all meant to be. This happened before my break down when I thought I had more or less healed from my childhood and had been gradually learning to trust and be open once again.

As I held her I realised she had known this was our last day together and had been trying to say good bye, but I hadn't listened, I had been too busy. I knew how psychic she and I were with each other but I had not listened to her, had not let her know that she was more important than planting a row of beans or pulling weeds - whichever it had been.

David helped me bury her when I could bear to let her limp body go and took me to a nursery to buy some plants to place over her body in the garden. He was so gentle with me and the grief passed. Just writing this a decade or more later I can feel her presence within me still.

Life is an experience in between birth and death, much of it suffering in one form or another, a basic simple truth for us all to ponder. How we deal with death and bereavement, how we face our own mortality depends so much on the culture within which we are born and will die too.

For me death is no tragedy – ever, it is just a matter of when, how, and where. For everything that lives this is the same reality.

Death and bereavement are a conversation we seriously need to have more of in the culture I have lived in.

It might just make us value life a little more in the process, our own and that of others too.

My friends, who all died of cancer, also all suffered a lot in that process, but Saffy didn't; she chose a quick exit when she knew she had done her time here.

We should all have that option made available to us as humans. We should all talk about death more openly and readily so that we are not afraid to live freely. Death is just a transition to another state of existence, it is only those left behind who are bereft, and our selfishness that we want our friend or beloved animal back.

But then I have them both whenever I want if I sit and think of them in my heart/mind.

Much has been written about the stages of bereavement we mostly go through, including grief, confusion and anger. Perhaps if we explored these realities as part of learning to live, they would not hurt us so much and be easier to bear. The bereavements I have experienced have taught me that so far but as I say I have yet to face a really huge impactful bereavement from a positive relationship.

Nothing is permanent, clinging on doesn't make it so. Finding ways to make the filling happy is worth the effort though, instead of worrying about the ending.

Bliss

First define bliss. Very difficult but here is my attempt.

I think it is such a unique experience that it cannot be adequately defined or described. As you read on you will also understand that I find it a pointless exercise, but for now let us come to some kind of shared understanding of what we are talking about.

My experience of bliss suggests it is the following - a state of complete harmony, a balance between inner and outer, a state of total peacefulness inner and outer, deepest happiness and contentment, love, and a delightful way to spend time in life. It is also perceptually illuminating, for seeing deeper truths without fear or attachment, for looking deeply into the true nature of reality and Interbeing.

I have known bliss in short brief glimpses and long stretches of time, lasting hours or in one case several months. Most people have some of these experiences at some point in their lives, some chemically induced and some naturally occurring either through meditation or as happened to me when I got well again after PTSD.

Bliss is what we all yearn for, one way or another, or rather we think that we do. Perhaps you might think again after reading this, perhaps not. Glimpses of bliss come from anywhere, from that moment when things just fall into place, a perfect moment shared with a profoundly loved one, a deeply connected post-coital embrace, holding one's own tiny new born in one's arms for the first time, watching a sunset or during or after a good meditation. These are moments of bliss that can be commonly found, but even then, not for all. They can equally be over-looked.

You cannot seek to experience that which you are not looking for, but it can come and hit you on the head.

The fleeting glimpses are like promptings, temptations, hints that there is more, that lead you on. They did me. They also helped me to stay alive; they gave me hope in a bleak early life; those few and fleeting moments when I was so present with what I was watching that everything disappeared, climbing trees and sitting in their tops, watching the world underneath and around me, and swaying gently with the wind, knowing that for this moment I was unreachable, 'unpunishable'.

I was completely unaware of the power of these moments until I started to learn meditation, many years later, and then I had occasional, stronger and more specific glimpses of the bliss state. I wanted them to take over, to remove the darkness. The more I chased after them, the more they were shy and evasive, retreating into the darkness of grasping and longing. In Buddhist terms, the more we are attached to finding them, the more they will evade us, non-attachment being the key to this search, goal-lessness being another.

With developing meditation and mindfulness skills, there is the bliss of finding you are fully grounded in the moment and can embrace the joyfulness of a single moment to its depth, but this kind of bliss often passes as soon as you become conscious of what you are feeling; as soon as you recognise what is happening it is gone like a flash. Again, it is the grasping and attachment that blocks the bliss and learning to let go.

And that is really the point to it. You cannot find bliss; it finds you if you are open to it. But is it what you really want?

I have been meditating for roughly quarter of a century at the point of writing this, and having mystical experiences for all of my life. These glimpses led me onwards, ever onwards, in search of something. I have written poetry, and other pieces that talk about this sense of searching.

The Bliss of a clear conscience.

If you are a deep practitioner of mindfulness you probably also embrace the ethical code attached to it. This is part of the Buddha's teachings for happiness, that of having a clear conscience. This form of bliss was hard won for me since I was filled with the guilt of my whole family and all their struggles. So, to find a path that led me to freedom from guilt, shame, and an overpowering burden of responsibility, this was free-ing and blissful indeed. Many people can find this form of bliss, but again it is not easy. It takes effort to shed the baggage, and to clear an overly developed sense of responsibility that is way beyond any realistic responsibility for anyone, let alone a child. We're only ever responsible for our own emotions and choices and behaviour in the present moment, and being blamed or blaming someone else is a pointless exercise. We have some duty to consider the needs of others too of course, it must never be all one sided. We all need to do our best to be our very best self and we all need to look at ourselves in honesty and not guilt or judgement and say 'where am I truly lacking and what can I do about this, how can I change myself for an even better version'. Being our best self brings bliss with it.

Bliss of acceptance

There is bliss of loving your life just exactly as it is, even though it may be about to change in ways you prefer it not to. Impermanence is a basic truth of life from which no one can escape. But so many people, including earlier versions of me, try to cling onto things which will always slip out of existence, whether it is a relationship that is now over, a status, a possession, a notion of something like security.

They are all illusions.

Once you can really let go of regrets and attachments and just allow 'what is' to sit in your hand and simply enjoy it while it is in your life, then you can find a state of bliss in the deep acceptance of this moment and the possibilities of change into the next one.

Bliss of MDMA and other chemicals

Well we have most probably all taken mind altering chemicals, caffeine, tobacco, alcohol, nicotine, cannabis, Valium, and they all have their part to play in human experience. I would add importantly that they never create a sustainable reality.

Reality is just you, at your basic un-intoxicated self, and this is only the fleeting realities of the moment.

However when you are in the really deep darkest place imaginable, which was how PTSD felt at times, unimaginably bleak and desolate, and filled with an unnamed and unrecognisable non- stop terror of everything except the tiny number of things that were safe (my husband David being the only real one) you are willing to become anything to escape, to release this suffocating nightmare that never ends. I knew all through my PTSD, and all through my life really, that this darkness was not who I am, it was something that happened to me, and it was not the sum of my life but for the moment it was all that existed in experiential terms.

The final phase or expression of my PTSD lasted six years in total although there were ebbs and flows during that time. It did result in a complete breakdown however, both of all the good things and all the bad, a complete clear-out of everything except my immediate family, David and the descendents (sounds like a new band name doesn't it lol).

He did a lot of online research about my problems because he had to watch me struggle to survive, hear me get up every night with insomnia and know that I was struggling to stay alive in each moment through each dark night and to trust that this too will end, that nothing is permanent.

So, he found the information about MDMA and how it had been developed originally to treat people with exactly my symptoms but due to ignorant political nonsense and irresponsible recreational use had been made illegal.

We got some, illegally, and just hoped it was a safe version, a risk worth taking since the alternative was becoming unthinkable. I took a little bit of it and felt stoned but nothing more. That same day for some reason I insisted David share it with me, so instead of him taking care of me whilst under the influence, we went to bed as a containment of the experience, and took some together.

When it kicked in, it was amazing, but only because it was us both sharing it together. On my own I felt chilled but not alive particularly. With David, it took us to a place where we could tangibly feel the amount of love that flowed between us both, it allowed us equally to open up to each other on a whole other level. We held each other in a painless embrace that was an endless deep connection, a 'marriage' on a whole other level, deeper than either of us ever imagined. It showed us how far reaching our love was when the fear was removed, and that is the point.

Remove all the layers of fear we each hold in our hearts and there is just love left.

We both were able to go to all the damaged, shameful, angry, frightened places we had never been able to do before and ordinary therapy would never have reached in either of us. It all came out, all the darkness and fear and desperation and desolation of my childhood, all the stories I had buried deeply as they were too painful to deal with back then. Him too. Now, wrapped in our beloved soulmate's arms they would be listened to and accepted and shared and released. We created stories of our younger selves, where they had met earlier on and been best friends instead of the rather lonely two children which we both once were. It worked.

Slowly and gradually it broke down the defensive high dark walls that surrounded me. Inch by inch they came down. When the MDMA wore off there were side effects to deal with each time but also a slowly increasing sense of potential liberation.

Then we decided enough was enough, the positives were slowing down and the side-effects of the come downs were getting harder to cope with, so after six sessions we decided we had come far enough via this route and it was back to the practice of meditation. The fear and darkness returned from time to time but it faded again and each time more quickly. The MDMA had broken the hard shell of darkness behind which I was totally trapped.

But I was not yet home free. I was ok as long as nothing triggered me. If it did, I locked down again. Less time delay before I came back each time but it was this endurance and fear of triggering that was getting me down all over again. How can you live a life when you are afraid of everything still triggering you? I couldn't go out without being with David. I had been so mashed by it all by this point that my resilience was wearing very thin and I just wanted out, in spite of the love I knew we shared. But the recognition of the deep bond between David and myself kept me going, I knew this was what was really true and the darkness was still something I just had to deal with.

I decided to do four mindfulness retreats in quick succession, over four months, and all with the Community of Interbeing in England and France at Plum Village. After each one, I felt the darkness finally and actually fully dissolve, bit by bit.

Things were happening that would have left me so shocked that I would have been catatonic, especially by an experience I had in someone's car on the way to the last of these retreats when I was verbally abused quite badly, and suddenly I coped with it.

I found myself detached from it, apart from what this person was doing to me, it was unreal. I asked to be let out of the car and that was refused so basically I had been kidnapped as well but that was ok.

I coped.

I survived and was ok.

That was when I knew it had finally gone. What happened next however was even more astonishing.

Bliss after PTSD

This was a facebook post I made just a couple of months later.

'Well here I am nowadays with some weird stuff happened in my brain, the PTSD has now finally and completely gone but so has most of everything else with it - so life is like floating in a large balmy lagoon with nothing to do except splash around and do what comes to mind, nothing seems to matter that much and things like emotions are so small and distant, except happiness which is huge and fills me up, and when I look down it is bottomless and when I look up, it is endless there too. It is the size of the universe and beyond. So who am I nowadays - really not sure but even that doesn't matter a jot any more - I think all those years of intensive meditation and mindfulness have paid off but not sure if there is a name for it lol - there - I just thought I would share with you all xxx and on that note, I think I will happily splash to the garden and float around with a weeding fork out there for a while before it all freezes over.' And I have to say that summed it up for over four months. I call it my time on golden pond or golden lagoon, because everything seemed to be bathed in a pale golden light and I felt suspended as if in water.

However, it was not all wonderful. It was affecting my beloved David because I had no connection to him or anything at all, no variation in emotional state at all, no attachment, no self to become attached with.

I commented on my experiences, but they left everyone out, not because of selfishness but because I didn't feel any specific attachment to anything.

All was part of me and me of it.

The trouble was that they did not feel that same experience, so we could not relate to each other.

I almost felt trapped in this other place away from them and I so wanted them to come and join me but I realised I had to come back to them instead.

Then the bliss got broken into by a single destructive act, by someone who did not realise what they were doing, like a terrorist breaking down and smashing their way into my heavenly place. But this place had started to feel more like a prison of even more loneliness, except that I couldn't feel anything except happiness, bliss. So, slowly, normal emotional states began to return.

Bliss of Contentment

It was then that I realised how valuable all emotional experiences are, how they give you variety and the glorious ups and downs of normal life, this simply is the point, the boring details of everyday life.

THIS IS IT

That Zen statement can sound very sensible, and down to earth, from a normal human consciousness point of view. It suddenly took on a whole new meaning now. The mundane suddenly became very precious and nothing was too small to be not worth bothering with. I realised what they say all along but until you get that sudden shocking insight, (that this is really all that matters, this moment, this experience, this love, this challenge.

It is all so wonderful, so rich and so interesting and varied,) it is just another teaching.

In that four months or so, bliss, although so delightful in many ways, insulated me from life completely and thus had become boring above everything else. It had become tedious, relentless and made all life pointless, valueless. When nothing matters you can fall into apathy, it doesn't matter, I don't care, etc.

Having the variation was so precious, so real, so alive, so intensely exciting that it seemed the lights were completely on above the present moment. All the rest was just a shadow, the past and future merely distant notions, a real effort to consider.

This moment is in the spotlight and everything else is just non-existent shadow really.

Perhaps being in the darkness for so long made the contrast so vivid and bright, perhaps the fact that I had probably had PTSD since I was about three yrs. old meant everything that had developed after that initial freezing moment, everything which had built up over my lifetime fell away with the PTSD when it went. I felt completely free of all of it, including a sense of self. A whole new level of bliss had developed. Any Ego that had built itself on the back of the frozen child had vanished with the melt.

Post Bliss

I feel almost normal again now, human normal I mean since that is in many ways the true abnormal. Life has its ups and downs, sometimes I still get triggered and have to wait for the darkness that nudges its way back into my life to ebb away again, but now I can clearly see my choices.

Each time I can choose not to let the darkness take me completely. There is still the moment before I am able to take that choice, when I am frozen once more. But that is even ok now. It is just my body, my amygdala still working to do its job of protecting me. My daily simple happiness is just bliss, that and still being madly in love with my amazing husband who stuck with me through this incredible journey.

Many would not have been able to do that for me. This year we reach twenty-one years of togetherness and we are more together than ever before; every moment is a celebration of everything we have shared and all the growing we have done together. Apparently, I have helped him as much as he has helped me. I don't see it quite, given my story, but I am glad that he feels that way too.

Bliss is slightly overrated though. It is fine for a few glimpses and seems like the most amazing thing that could happen to you. But don't go after it, just enjoy the moments you have. That is true mindfulness from the heart. I still love meditating even though I still struggle with it with my ADHD and restless body, but none of that matters any more. This moment is all that is real, just this never-ending happy glorious loving moment. Everything else is irrelevant. That is bliss, the normal ups and downs, the good and bad, the drama and the tedium that is all bliss. It really is. The deep bedrock of bliss that underpins my every moment means that although the surface can at times be really ruffled and stormy, beneath I can always touch that base of truth in reality or bliss

Lessons from the Lagoon of contentment

Since coming back from the lagoon I have regular insights into the nature of reality and what it is. Sometimes I have a conversation with a friend and I realise that I have a completely new understanding of whatever it is we are talking about, some deeper, finer points of spiritual philosophy. In the time of experiencing being part of everything, being in the cosmic soup of reality, I 'know' things instinctively which I later recognise I know intellectually too, but the two are not linked.

They are part of the same experience but the intellect is deeply limited by its own recognition of itself, i.e. its ego nature. This other knowing is way beyond that. It is not self-aware but purely experiential.

It is only in these conversations that I am reminded of ideas that I once held that have now dissolved in the face of that reality. The 'this is it' is mostly about how to live life in the present moment and embrace it in all its messy glory, but it goes beyond that too. 'This is it' means that the material world is the spiritual world too; there is no separation between them, other than the discriminatory mind of humankind, the ego. There is no separate soul or spiritual energy.

That lagoon was all that there is, ALL that there is, spiritual and material is one too just as we are all one. Immediately you try to separate out the spiritual from other you are into duality and that is missing the point. Consciousness is equally in everything, it is already there in its entirety, in the material of the substance which makes up everything. It cannot be apart from that. Everything that is material is equally spiritual and like-wise in reverse. To separate them out is to miss the point. There is no evolution as a progression of awareness, it is already there. The ego is what separates us from the understanding; the symbolism of the myth of the fall from Eden is that awareness of self which separates us from everything. If we see self and other, then we are in duality. It is not learning or developing that is needed, there is no evolution of consciousness, there is simply waking up.

The biggest difficulty in trying to write about this is that words themselves cannot convey the experience of everything all at once all the time without beginning or ending, the true meaning of eternity. You can think about it and know about it, but you cannot be in it until you let go of the ideas that keep you separate from it. We train children to be apart from it, we socialise their brains into the ego self-understandings of me and other. We call this normal development, de-individuation.

The child is born experiencing mother and self as one. We teach it separation, individual identity, duality.

We take this away from each and every child that is born in this world because we are so trapped by duality ourselves that we think that is the true nature of reality.

The consciousness, which is in my body, is in all the cells in my body. The cells in my body are made of molecules that exist everywhere too, in each other living creature, carbon, oxygen, hydrogen, iron, calcium and so on. These atoms have the consciousness in them.

The arrangement of them into a form that I identify as Sylvia means that I have that consciousness in all of my body.

When I die, that consciousness is not separate from those molecules. It stays within each molecule because it is not separate from it, so that when the form of this body disintegrates in decrepitude of old age and death, the consciousness in each cell and atom of this body will become something else, another form of existence. That consciousness is not more or less than it ever was, it is all that there ever was and all that there ever will be.

Self-improvement is not getting 'better' but rather in stripping away all the misinformation that we convince ourselves is reality. Spiritual evolution is not about gaining a higher understanding; it is recognising how erroneous our previous understanding of existence was. The main resistance to this is 'being right', having too much invested in our individual self-nature as we see it so that we cannot let go of those ideas and beliefs and that is suffering, that is the nature of suffering. The blindness of suffering is the blindness of self-awareness which we think gives us so much specialness as a species and as an individual.

My ego self still governs me to some extent, and I really don't mind that. It has joy and suffering in its undulations of experience, but when I let it go again, when I detach from it through meditation, then I am in touch with the numinous nature of existence and I know that nothing is separate.

There is no loss or gain, there is no you and me, there is just a lagoon of pure consciousness of which we are all a part, a reality of which we only need to wake up to.

How can one not have deep gratitude for experiences that led to this understanding, however grueling they might have been?

Bliss can come in so many forms but chasing it will never allow it to manifest - so unfold your defenses and find it within yourself.

Boundaries

We all need boundaries for self protection. We are not emotional or physical machines, and we need to protect ourselves occasionally. However, boundaries should not be mistaken for defenses.

A true boundary is flexible, internal and is based on your own deepest, ego-free, Interbeing based values of what you will and will not allow yourself to be forced into or subjected to. It allows other people to be who they need to be and for all to be 'whom' they are without anybody encroaching on anybody else's wellbeing. A boundary says I love you and I know you love me and I accept your right to be who you are and you accept my right to be who I am; if you need to do this and I need to not do this that is all ok, we can listen deeply to each other but we can agree to differ without fear and anger getting in the way.

A barrier on the other hand is rigid and rule based. It says if you love me you will obey this rule or do that in order to suit me or please me. In children it can create approval junkies. It allows little or no flexibility and creates division and separation. A barrier is a form of avoidance, it says 'don't go there - don't do this - because you are afraid'. It encourages the build-up of fear-based restrictions in your life.

Barriers want to silence you or others without listening or being open. Barriers want to:

- stop you acting and hide you away,
- protect you from the things in life which you most need to face related to truth and compassion and living ethically and free of harmful outcomes for yourself
- hide you away and pretend it has your best interests at heart, it will stop you facing your fear full on and overcoming it

- keep you afraid and cowering.

Barriers come from fear and boundaries come from strength, trust and openness, and confidence in your value system.

A little while ago a friend told me not to talk about things that caused her distress. Yet her behaviour and choices were contributing to those events occurring and her avoidance of the deeper issues have, and continue to have, a contribution to the devastating impacts on the lives of other people. The friendship feels as if it is slipping out of existence because barriers do that, and boundaries do not. Her barriers of self-defense are unable to flow with my boundaries and values in life anymore and she is closing down in defense against me. I remain open to her if at any time in the future she feels able to listen to me again, as I have done with her many times before. But I have my boundaries relating to my conscience of the greater good in life and one of them is that I will not collude with abuse of others in any form or guise if I can avoid it. I will not judge others who do, but I will always speak out about it.

A word of warning here though, whatever your values and boundaries are, do not fall into the trap of self-righteousness about being right and others wrong. That is just another form of barrier making you feel better at someone else's expense.

My other tradition is Quaker and one of the favourite advices I follow repeatedly is 'have you considered you may be mistaken'.

So, in this case am I wrong to challenge or to question my friend's choices or is it a positive thing that has short term challenges to deal with.

My answer to that is to look deeply at motivation. My motivation is not to be right but to help to alleviate suffering and challenge choices of behaviour that contribute to it.

My value says I cannot please other people at the expense of ignoring my vow not to contribute to the suffering in the world any more than I do.

I will also enable myself to lessen that as quickly as I am able to by re-educating myself about it all.

I feel like I am being even more self-righteous and 'right' here but I honestly promise that this is not my intention, I am just trying to break down the complex links in separating our ego-based barriers and healthy enabling boundaries.

For instance, in my life someone proudly announced they were having all their traditional internal pine doors replaced by deeply polished new mahogany doors that all matched. Their house extension meant that period pine painted doors no longer matched the newer ones and she wanted uniformity and no more painting to do. I could not conceal my obvious shock and horror at her refusal to acknowledge that her choices had immense impact on the forests where these trees grow and that this was a wasteful and unnecessary use of natural resources. My deep distress was impacted by the short story I had recently read by one of my favourite authors, Isabel Allende, about the lives of indigenous tribes-people from the amazon forests and the brutal and inhumane impact on their lives by the logging companies, turning them into either sex-slaves as comfort women or labouring-slaves as tree fellers. I could clearly see the connection between these two realities, that connection caused me deep distress - and she was angry with me for bringing it to her attention and didn't see why I should be upset or impinge on her lifestyle with my tales of nasty things that were not her responsibility.

Another incident recently also occurred in a similar way when a friend of mine was annoyed that I don't have an I-Phone and then was even more annoyed with me for stating the reason why I don't have an I-phone.

It is because of the harmful waste of enslaved children's lives and often their deaths in the mining for the minerals that these products depend upon.

I won't get an I-phone until this changes and all the mining is done by adults, willingly, safely, and ecologically soundly.

If we separate these two examples out into stages of processing for differences between boundaries and barriers.

First of all, we have an underlying value, in this case mine is not to cause or inflict suffering onto others knowingly, if I can possibly help it, and as far as I am able, to also work to end the causes of that self-same suffering for others.

That is a deep core value I hold and cannot be diverted from. If I am diverted from that value, then I feel so at odds with myself and my core being that it causes me deep distress. Sometimes I have no choice and am compromised, as we all are.

This core value can be anything that you feel strongly about for your own sense of ethical, spiritual or moral well-being. Going against this value causes me deep distress because I feel the suffering of all those individuals trapped in those horrendous circumstances. I do not want to be a part of that system of enslavement and cruelty by contributing to a market that demands these products at these costs. So, this is the part that is self-interested if you like, I want to feel happy in my life, not sad all the time, thus I have values that allow this to occur. I almost certainly have a lot of mirror neurons which make me deeply empathetic and sensitive, but I find strength in that sensitivity and do not run from it if I can help it. The strength is in speaking out and helping to co-create changes to end that kind or level of suffering.

Then we have the choices made, deeper knowledge we can all develop, our understanding of our place in the universe.

It is not all up to us! Shock Horror, what does this mean?

We are but simply a part of everything that exists, a very important part of it all but not the only part.

We need to establish safe boundaries for our small part. The ego will try and keep you at the centre of everything; 'it is all down to you, all your responsibility to rescue the world and sort it all out, and with some urgency'. Thus we are tempted to draw up the barriers and protect ourselves and hide from these imposed 'truths' which are in fact misunderstandings. But if we do go into denial mode, this is denying that we are part of it all, and thus is harmful to our sense of self, isolating us. So we find other people who will collude with our denials. In legal terms this is 'willful blindness' but it is one of the most common failings of humanity. We must stay open and aware and have good strong, carefully considered interrelated boundaries; we can all embrace this approach, fully based on the Buddhist ethics teachings of mindfulness, instead.

Nothing is resolved in shutdown mode.

You cannot really run away from anything, because you are part of everything and it is part of you, thus it will impinge on you at some time or another, in some form or another. And if you only have barriers to protect you, they will be washed away, like all flood defenses ultimately are, by the torrents of the truth.

Your best choices, decisions and boundaries are those made in full awareness, knowing that it is not all down to you. You cannot avoid however, taking your part in either making it worse (actively contributing is little different to a head in the sand) or ameliorating the unkind world situations.

We have some choices, even if they may be limited. People will need, for instance, an I-phone in order to carry out their business lives.

They can also campaign and sign petitions to state they want this slavery practice changed and these abuses to be stopped and viable alternatives used instead.

That is within everyone's power to do, and enough people together create a flood of protest that does actually mean these practices are ended, perhaps not overnight but in time. The people who have vested interests in hiding these horrors will put up many barriers to prevent themselves being compromised and losing their source of exploitation, but we can collectively create a torrent of protest against such practices and thus bring about change. Torrents of truth always over-come barriers because barriers are rooted in fear and truth will always overcome fear in the end.

Barriers lack the flexibility to withstand truths.

Boundaries work with truths.

The illusion of time can make us feel cynical of this statement, but if you explore in depth you can see it does always happen. It is the failure of immediate outcomes that leads to cynicism and doubt, taking the long view shows it is always real though.

We have a clear boundary and can maintain our values but also be pragmatic about our role in the whole picture. This way the ego does not get over important and take control again in a different format.

Stepping back and understanding the universe as being basically made of molecules; just energy and particles organised in specific ways. We cannot destroy or create anything, but we can have a say in how that matter is organised. Knowing this and keeping this in mind can be very liberating and empowering but keeping it in mind means responding also to the reality of a material world that we also all live in and are obliged to interact with. It is the marriage of those two realities that enables us to develop strong values and boundaries that keep us safe.

Everything can be changed, nothing is permanent, and we can influence those changes by our own energetic inputs.

It is worth the effort, and cynicism is not necessary.

Just don't think it is going to happen in an instant, or even in your lifetime which is no more than a blink of an eye anyway.

But your input via your energy and active rejection of cruelty and abuses will and does create change in the end. Don't let go of that bit, in the end. There is a time to speak out and protest and a time to be simply happy and in touch with the pure loving joy of life itself. By not being part of the problem, you automatically become part of the solution.

Finally, in this process, learn to let go of the ego centric view of the world, and your place in it, by taking firm hold of a realistic assessment of how much is your responsibility. You can only be responsible for the choices you take in this present moment. So, no matter which choices you made in the past you can always change them NOW and work to undo what you may have done in the past, or at least not repeat them and add to the burdens of suffering in this world. If you know in your heart that these things are true of yourself then you have developed natural boundaries which are strong and solid and will keep you 'safe' from your inner critic. Because that is probably who you most fear, the inner critic who will use someone else to prove they are right and that you are not as great as you thought you were or want to be. Which leads to another important part of healthy boundary building; be honest and also pragmatic about yourself. You are probably great to some people and yuk to others, with a lot of in-betweens. I think of myself as Marmite, some love me, and some can't stand me- and that is completely fine with me. This is a spectrum and none of it is accurate because no-one can know you from the outside. Even if they can read your energy, they can only know you at some level.

Let's face it, we don't even know ourselves very well and we are party to all the thoughts and motivations going on inside our own minds. Sometimes others can know things about you that you don't know about yourself, and visa versa.

They can see what our 'egos' would have us avoid looking at, but they don't know all of you either, or you them.

We are all enigmas and that is because we are not fixed. We may change our values over time, based on what we learn. We will almost certainly adapt our choices and behaviours over time too, based on feedback and self-image and many other factors. So how can anybody deeply know the entirety of another when they are always evolving? If you can accept this about yourself you can give yourself room to change, remove the need to be right or not found out, remove all guilt and shame and become an emotionally flexible but strong person with very healthy boundaries. Believe me this takes time and effort and I cannot claim to have mastered it yet although I am using this process and it has certainly worked over the years alongside other principles such as acceptance, gratitude and letting go.

We all want to appear to be strong and unassailable, but real strengths arise out of openness, and not being afraid of our vulnerability or our depth of emotion. Real strength comes from having firm boundaries, which are not rigid; that you will not compromise but are open to modification if that fits with the original core value.

For instance, I might change my stance on mahogany if it can be demonstrated clearly how the new way of managing its harvest involves no habitat loss on devastating scales and no harm to other living beings apart from the trees themselves of course, which are also living beings with consciousness (another essay elsewhere).

Healthy boundaries allow us to laugh off the nonsense coming our way daily without being unkind about it, and without defending ourselves; there is no need to defend if one is not afraid.

Another minor point is that there are times when we have to say, 'I can't manage this right now'. My own example is that I am still recovering from a breakdown caused by PTSD.

This has been the most devastating experience of my life and in other ways the very best, because so many good things came out of it. But I do still get triggered by anything that echoes the energy that caused the PTSD in the first place. And thus, I often say 'no- can't do that'.

However, I never say 'no I can't do that ever', just 'not yet', or 'not all of those things in one go'. Step by step I am finding I can cope with slightly more each day, a little more risk, a little more full on activity, a little more demand and expectation, never allowing too much but always remaining flexible to the expanding level of what I can cope with and how my nervous system is gradually rewiring itself.

This flexibility, withdrawal and pushing myself makes a healthy boundary, not a barrier. There's no silence, no refusal, just cautious recalibration of what I can manage today.

One of the really great outcomes of the PTSD was that all my defenses were smashed in the torrent of terror and truthful realisations that overcame me. I've been very careful not to allow them to re-assemble as they were but instead, I sit back and re-examine everything I have learned through my practice of mindfulness.

I've worked to establish healthy boundaries and I remain open and do not allow the energy of defensiveness to reassemble in my emotional landscape, after all that was exactly what let me down so badly when I got broken.

My boundaries grow stronger by the day, backed up by the evolving neuro-plasticity of a strong mindfulness practice. I am looking forward to how that works out, tomorrow and next week and next year - who knows how far ahead.

Developing a healthy boundary for your core values in life keeps you safe and free, and stops you being defensive and possibly pushing others away.

Change

Change is something that happens to us all. It is not something anybody can avoid but people – we - I - do all we can to stop it happening sometimes and then are frustrated by how slowly the other changes we think we want to happen actually occur. So embracing change requires courage, patience and acceptance, the ability to go with the flow, to be adaptable, to allow yourself to evolve with life as it evolves around you.

'To resist or not to resist that is the question', or as the Borg once said, 'resistance is futile'.

Well perhaps it is and perhaps it isn't. You may hold back time and change on one level but the cost to yourself may be far greater than going with the flow. We recently had to make a huge change in our own lives, which was to sell up our beloved house and retreat centre because we just could not manage the sheer physical enormity of its maintenance any more. The house had become a burden. We could have resisted for quite a while longer, but it would have done us more damage emotionally, physically, and possibly as a couple too. We got out when we needed to, and it was deeply painful and traumatic but necessary. Our beloved house had also taken on the role of persecutor, burden, nightmare!

I struggled massively also because the whole process in itself was a nightmare at a time of great uncertainty with BREXIT and all sorts of other chaos going on around. Not least of which was the loss of three very important people in our lives to cancer within a few months of each other- just before and after moving date.

Change happens all the time.

❖ Change happens to our bodies, cell by cell as they die, are repaired, replaced, and age Sometimes our own cells even turn against us as in cancer.

❖ Change happens in our lives, often just by events occurring, sometimes we pursue changes and sometimes we want to avoid them, but they happen anyway, changes in jobs and where we live, changes in circumstances of all kinds

❖ Change happens in our intimate relationships – sometimes the whole relationship ends and a new one begins but sometimes it is just as a relationship develops and matures it will change anyway, just because we change, and our circumstances change.

❖ Changes in family and friendships as people are born and die, become ill, move away, move on, fall out.

❖ Changes in belief - less common overall but still happens, from the dramatic Paul on the Road to Damascus shock awakening to the opposite, when we gradually walk away from the beliefs we were given in childhood and choose to find our own path. Many people find that over time their experiences shift their beliefs from one position to another even if in roughly the same area, such as religion. Someone recently said to me how much their experiences of God had changed the way they thought and talked about God in the present. I could relate to that change in perception or belief. My own relationship with the concept of God has shifted massively throughout my own life according to my experiences.

❖ Changes through experience - even if it is as basic as developing aversion to a food that has made us very ill- that is still a development in our life, a change that we might not even consider or notice. Sometimes the changes hurt us and force us to look at ourselves or become victims and sometimes the experiences are positive and teach us that we can trust and love each other openly.

Some people like to say, 'Oh I will never change' or 'he /she will never change', but you see they will even if they don't notice it. We are all changing every day, every moment.

So here comes the choice we all have to make.

We can either embrace changes on all levels or we can avoid them.

All I know from personal experience is that if I avoid any kind of changes, I will pay a price for that, and if I embrace them, I benefit massively.

Sometimes it is difficult to see what choices we are being given.

Sometimes doors are simply slammed in our face and nothing appears to be opening up for us elsewhere. This can feel very disheartening and rejecting, but it is also a point of growth in trust that the right door will open at the right time.

I have had periods of time when it felt like every door was slamming shut on me. Much of this was during the six-year period of my breakdown with PTSD. I lost so much of what I thought was my life at the time. I lost a huge number of people because I just could not cope with their inability to understand my illness and I could not communicate with them in ways than enabled me to feel safe.

Post Traumatic Stress Disorder is basically when one's nervous system is so overloaded that it cannot process any more ups and downs, plus you react in dramatic 'over the top' ways to everything and cannot control it, you feel terror at the slightest thing - 0 to millions in one second. I cannot sleep because my body is so locked into rigidity of fear and if you do sleep you wake in a state of shock and terror, in my case gasping in shock, or often screaming or crying out loudly.

I don't blame anyone for not coping with me. Being told to pull myself together or keep quiet did not help at all, they made me feel more afraid.

I also lost my chance at achieving a PhD, for which I had a bursary and a lot of enthusiasm as it had been a long term goal, but even on the descent down into the real maelstrom of my illness I was failing to cope, I could not take anything in, my memory could not work, my brain could not think. I lost that dreamed for opportunity.

At first, I resisted the breakdown and did everything I could to hold myself together. I sort of succeeded for a while, but a number of smaller incidents impacted on me disproportionately and it just continued to pile onto me until I had to stop holding on and just let it happen.

I let the breakdown take me with it and watched as my life and my sense of self was entirely dismantled, apart from my sons and husband and a very small number of really deep friends.

To survive it at all I had to find ways of practicing and holding onto the truths as I knew them. That nothing is permanent, that this too will pass. That this is just another even more powerful transition in my life than I ever went through before, that this is happening to me but is not who I am.

As I came out of the breakdown, I realised I'd changed in more ways than I could enumerate. I am not sure if I'd resisted any less at the beginning it would've made much difference, but it would've possibly prevented many of the fallout losses which occurred, though I now accept them as just what happened then, and this is now.

So, change can engulf us or chip us along more gradually. Don't let the dramatic nature of my breakdown put you off though. What I have gained is massive. I can honestly say I'm profoundly grateful for those insights into some of the most wonderful life lessons, much of which I now write about.

How do we embrace changes?

First of all, you have to be able to look at yourself and recognise how perfectly imperfect you already are at any given moment, but without judgment.

We are often taught that ultimately, we are all already perfect, and we just need to let go of the imperfections that sully our lives. Those imperfections are my valuable teaching tools and maybe for those around us. Don't forget, without the very unskillful people around me that led to my complete breakdown, I would not have got to where I am now and that would be a shame.

I could still be upset or angry about my own life story. It was tough to live through it all, but others have it worse of course too. I don't think any of it was intended but simply arose out of unskilfullness or emotional ignorance.

When we are unskillful or unaware in our actions and behaviours, it can cause great damage in the short term. But if the recipient can turn that to their advantage, then we have cause to feel gratitude for their, or our own, unskilfulness in the first place.

I can now say I am grateful for the experiences because through changing how I thought about them, I reclaimed them for my own advantage.

Resistance to change can cause one of the biggest psychological and spiritual self harm states of mind, Victimhood, to which I have given its own entire chapter.

If I'd resisted the changes needed to turn my life around, I could still be a very damaged and depressed individual. Thankfully I am not.

But briefly speaking if we are unable to embrace change and accept our life events as they unfold, to make positive use of them through growth and development of our own inner states.

Then we are likely to feel cheated, hard done by, confused, lost, and quite probably angry. This is all self harm.

SO be open to self exploration in the first place, go deeply if you can, but in stages which enable you to make progress. The world and all its people are your mirror; they will tell you all that you need to know, in stages, about what to change and what to develop. One of the greatest gifts my husband gave me throughout our marriage is his willingness to be as blunt and honest with me as I am with him, and not to let anything slip by unnoticed if it can be useful as a point of change.

This mutual mirroring has simply strengthened our relationship and improved it vastly.

Mostly it required that we both hear things we did not like or want to hear at first, until we got used to this process. We developed our own strategies for coping with those more upsetting early confrontations. But we also learned we could trust that feedback, that spousal mirror was a fair and wise one, and ultimately very accepting and gentle too, supporting the changes in process. This is the opposite of the usual 'tit-for-tat', 'well you did this' to which the other party rejoins 'well you did that'.

When you decide to make a change in yourself you will not suddenly magically manage this new version of you. It will be like learning to walk, so don't spank the toddler in you going through this process, that is unkind. Encouragement and forgiveness of slip-ups, as the old habits fight against its replacements.

To get into practice, start by making small changes in your daily life. Change habits and routines as far as you are able to. Eat and drink more mindfully. Move more mindfully too, more in tune with your own body and its needs to care and maintenance.

Speak with more consideration and forethought if you can, to consider the impact your words may have on another without you ever realising it.

I find this particularly difficult as I also have ADHD which makes me very prone to just pointing things out. This one for me is also about the hardest, because if I am at all anxious, I just blurt things out and have had to forgive myself so many times for this slip, whilst recognising that although I am working on it, I will probably never get it mastered. Repairing the damage done can also be more difficult. But I am rarely unkind with it, just perhaps too open or honest or blunt.

Trying to pin your life down to exactly what you think you want it to be can be another important thing to change. It is all very well to make a life plan, but can you respond to what happens when it doesn't work out as you intended? What if the resistance and determination you put into making life as you think it should be is actually stopping something far more wonderful from manifesting. You are blocking your own happiness with your own planning.

So yes, go ahead and think what you want to do, and then put some effort into that and see how it comes back, but be open to shifting your expectations and intentions according to the patterns they create when they unfold. I could stay very angry about how I had it all set up to finally do my PhD and my horrible breakdown came along and smashed it all up. OR as I do say, I learned so many wonderful things from the time I spent following that particular dream and those outcomes are sufficient and now form part of how I am moving on into different avenues. Which narrative would lead to more happiness and possibly more life adventures and which to unhappiness and bitterness?

Like all these chapters, each one overlaps with many others, but recognising that change should and must be a part of your approach to life is really, really important, crucial even, to finding deep happiness for the rest of your life.

One final advantage I have found to embracing life changes, is that it is far less stressful, less anxiety making, less challenging. You do not have to keep all the balls in the air at once, you can let them drop and see how that affects life. You can take the long view and wait to find out what the gift in everything actually is. You can embrace the changes in your own body as it ages, the changes in your own life as they evolve, and the changes in other people as they too evolve in their own stories. Just go with the flow and enjoy the journey. Life doesn't last that long anyway so don't waste a moment of it being stuck in the wrong place. And that brings me neatly onto the next C, embrace change by being compassionate with yourself too.

Compassion

Compassion is the basis of true love and feels as if it instinctively comes from the heart. If it comes purely from thought, then it risks automatically being controlled by the vagaries of mind or ego. You cannot then 'act' compassionately, even if you do feel compassion.

Compassion is not sympathy, which is patronising and based on a position of 'me up, you down' and 'I feel sorry for you and your suffering'. I find sympathy a most uncomfortable experience.

Compassion is not empathy either, which is about your own experience being transposed onto someone else's experience. I used to get this one wrong a lot, and people have got it wrong with me too.

Empathy is when someone uses their own experience to tell 'the other' they understand their experience, and to inform them of how they think they might be feeling, based on their own experiences, and in reverse of course.

Sometimes it may work, bringing you both closer through a shared experience, a bond built on shared suffering, but that is a tenuous basis for any relationship and may not last too long as one of you will almost certainly move forwards and the shared sense of victimhood will dissolve. And that is the other problem with both sympathy and empathy – they suggest victims, victimhood, and a possible tendency to wallow in suffering. That blocks true healing and constricts the movement required for change and growth.

Compassion allows the other one to speak without being told what they should think or feel differently - UNLESS they have asked you for guidance or advice. Only then is it appropriate to respond with anything other than a deep listening to hear how much they are suffering.

Making 'appropriate' faces can appear very false, as indeed they are; even without words we can convey sympathy and empathy and 'I know what you are feeling' attitudes.

Instead deeply listening is what most people need, and compassion is expressed in this way, no need for facial gymnastics or carefully placed comments which bring it back to you. And no judgments.

However, there are times when compassion will make us speak out!

If we can hear how much someone is self harming with their thought trains, compassion does allow us to make suggestions of alternatives, to reframe their situation back to them, to show them the positives they might gain from the situation without denying how much it is hurting them.

The Buddha taught that to know all is to forgive all. I have found that to be true on a personal level too. Once we can understand how someone else might feel, probably based on our own experiences but without it being about our experiences, we can start to forgive them for their mistakes in life and have compassion for them instead.

Once we start to come from a place of compassion for others, then we can feel compassion for ourselves too.

And vice versa of course!

Compassion builds on itself. You cannot force or create it. You cannot choose to develop it. It develops naturally through the gradual letting go of our own ego and our own need to be in the picture at all times, to be right, to be good, to be seen to be good.

A lot of people talk about compassion, about how they see its importance, about how they explore it, but there is something about them that is still 'all about self' and not other, thus it is not compassion and the ego has hijacked the concept for its own enhancement.

Compassion is an essential quality for the spiritual path. Some people act out the spiritual path behaviours and bypass their own development by talking about compassion but not practicing it at all.

My first experience of true and overwhelming compassion was when I was coming out of my own final and worst PTSD breakdown. I had been on the receiving end of massive amounts of compassion from my husband who got me through that illness like nobody and nothing else could have done. He allowed me to be ill, he knew I was working on getting well again all the time and that it would take time to heal. He allowed me that time without any sign of frustration. When I have asked him about it since he said he knew I was working as hard as I could using my mindfulness and spiritual understanding to self heal, and he wanted me to come back to him. So I did.

Experiencing that level of compassion was an amazing expression of true love and helped me to accept that I was loved and loveable and that my parents might have been wrong about me, the cause of my breakdown. Compassion was completely unknown when I was growing up and that lack took its toll on all of us. That is why I am so passionate about developing love and compassion in myself nowadays but through the release of my ego and its demands. We never get rid of the ego completely but through a practice of mindfulness and meditation, we can diminish its power over us and its control of our behaviour.

We can develop compassion for our ego. I did this and found it much easier to do less of the self punishing, self judging and self criticising. Our ego is only trying to do its own thing and once we recognise it is not who we are but just a child trying to control our life and make sense of it all, we can give it a hug and say don't bother, life happens anyway.

The ego is a child needing reassurance and love and yes compassion too.

So if occasionally it still bounces out of control, once you wake up to that fact then re-assure it everything is fine, it will calm down again and be less likely to jump up and take over in the future.

A sense of humour is required in self – compassion. The ego takes everything far too seriously and wants to be right in everything. If we can take a loving look at life instead of harsh and judgmental viewpoints, then we can make more room for compassion on all sides, because there is always a bigger story and a wider perspective than the one that we see alone, no matter what.

Humans are prone to something called the fundamental attribution error. This is what makes us judgmental and lack compassion. It is the basis on which we judge others to be at fault in their character if they mess up in some way, but we of course are not lacking any personality at all and are always pushed into a course of behaviour by circumstance beyond our control.

That is the biggest mistake we all make as humans in how we view each other. The truth lies somewhere in between. We are all controlled by external forces and internal drivers. We are all capable of learning how to manage and develop the better dimensions of who we each are, even though we will never please all of the people all of the time.

We are each responsible for that self-development, but we may not be responsible for lack of guidance from others, and thus not even realise we can do this kind of self development to reveal our best selves. The main advantage of this work is we can then feel a lot better about ourselves and stop running away from who we are inside, through drugs, alcohol, food, all other addictions, including projections onto others of our self hatred.

Compassion with self considers that we might not have understood the implications of our actions previously but by messing up we can learn from them.

That is the compassionate way forward for self and others. Once people see how kindness and compassion give you a more truly fulfilling life and deeper self acceptance in place of arrogance and pride (which constantly needs propping up) they make that choice willingly.

Acceptance is crucial to compassion, accepting that sometimes you and other people will mess up, occasionally big time, and appear to behave appallingly.

I can look back and see times when people would have thought that of me. What they could not see was that I was barely hanging together inside and was determined not to let that show on the outside because I had grown up in a world of no compassion and total jeering judgement of even the smallest mistakes. So defensively I didn't let people know how bad I felt inside and externally I thrashed around trying to cope and get to safer ground, to rebuild my life where I thought it would flourish best next. That happened to me about three times or more. Should I judge that person who I used to be as a bad person or have compassion for the level of suffering she carried around inside her all the time? The answer should be obvious given the title of this essay.

But I didn't. Even though I knew I was struggling to stay alive on a daily basis. I also piled on the internal judgements against myself until I had depressive breakdowns, small ones to begin with until the big one that came with Post Traumatic Stress Disorder.

My father was the principle originator of my PTSD and subsequent breakdown, goaded on, aided and abetted by my mother.

And in the midst of all the emotions that came flooding to the surface was a realisation that my mother also felt like this on the inside for her whole life, that she had given me the energy that lived inside her and that had been passed onto her by her parental generation also.

She'd also been traumatised in childhood and had lived with the dark energy of PTSD eating her away from the inside for her whole life.

How desperate she must have felt all her life and how much it must have truly hurt her to know that three children and seven grand children all avoided her as much as possible.

She had no compassion for herself so how could she have any compassion for me growing up as her eldest child. And inside she lived in complete darkness, which she projected onto me in an attempt to alleviate her own suffering because that is what humans in pain do to each other. She had no other way to tell her story than by passing it on to me, somehow unconsciously knowing that one day I would tell it for her.

In that moment of stark realisation, when no 'me' was present, I felt total and overwhelming compassion for her so that it filled me with grief for the sadness of her life. Then I knew true compassion, forgiveness and even gratitude in that moment, so deeply that it blew me away. Then I was able to let her go and all my own hurt and anger dissolved too.

Compassion must be when you let go of yourself

Compassion flows of its own accord, but there are meditations that enable us to cultivate an attitude of compassion and work towards this as part of our practice. In Thich Nhat Hanh's Plum Village tradition, of which I am a devoted student, it is called 'loving kindness meditation'.

You conjure up in your mind several people, someone you love unconditionally, someone neutral to you and someone you have difficulty with, and you generate thoughts and feelings of loving kindness for each of them equally, then yourself.

The first time I did this about twenty years ago I ran out of the room when it came to giving this to myself. It was inconceivable that I could behave lovingly in any way towards myself.

Travelling the Alphabet Emotionally

Once I had realised how much of my mother's dark energy of self-hatred was still stored inside me, which I felt from my childhood, I set to work to clear it.

It took years and a complete breakdown, but I am getting there. More or less.

Eventually mindfulness and the practices of TNH and the Plum Village community got me to a place of deep happiness for which I am eternally grateful.

BUT without my mother I would not have recognised the incredible value of compassion, how important it is, how essential it is for well balanced loving people in the world. I am so grateful to my mother for what she led me to and how she showed me the importance of this lesson.

In astrology terms I have a grand cross in my chart, which means life will be hard.

Some people don't make it through, but I did, and compassion is now my way of life. The only time it gets knocked out of me is when I get triggered and my old fear-based PTSD 'shut down' kicks in. Then I lose compassion for myself and others and become defensive once more. I work my way back from that as quickly as I can.

It is a dark place and my reminder of what my mum lived with forever. It is also a reminder of where I will go back to if I do not keep up this journey into compassion.

I could write endlessly about how important compassion has become in my own life but hope I have said enough for anyone reading this to also recognise how it would help them and anybody else in their life too, but also to recognise what compassion is not, and how tenuous it is to discover it deeply.

Depression - Taming the Black Dog

When I was a child, at interview for a secondary school, about ten or eleven yrs old, I was asked what I wanted to be when I grew up. I said actress.

A few years later on at school I said I wanted to be a writer when I grew up. Later on I said a poet too.

Both came true.

However!

With all three I got derision from teachers and or school 'friends' and some punishment from my mother who thought I should follow a stable career like teaching.

She had little imagination, but I swallowed my aspirations and tried office type jobs and then became a teacher for 16 yrs. Teaching is like acting though, being on stage to inspire your students to love your subject as much as you do. I think I managed this with some of them.

However, my greatest acting role was not letting anybody see how desperate I always was on the inside throughout my childhood – never let anyone see my vulnerability because, especially at home with my parents, it is just not safe to do so. Later in life the same applied to my siblings, never let them see you are vulnerable; the jeering or patronising sympathy would be awful.

Depression dogged me through much of the first four decades of my life, but I know this experience called depression is also different for all of us. It is recognised as a clinical condition and is not something you can shake off easily at all. When you are in it, it is appallingly real and all encompassing; it blots out all the light.

So why?

If you read other chapters you will come to recognise that mine was not a happy or easy childhood and I was often described as sullen, sulky, and moody by my parents. Actually I was despairingly depressed as a child, desperately so. I remember as a teen reading Steve Smith's poem 'Not waving but drowning' and realised that poetry could really speak to me about life experiences. That is now the poetry I write too.

> *I was much too far out all my life*
> *And not waving but drowning. (Stevie Smith)*

Think about those lines, don't they just sum it up. They certainly did for me.

Our perceptions are self-orientated. They are our interpretations of what is out there in the world. People see what they want to see in us. It often has little to do with our true nature and has everything to do with their perceptual clarity, or lack of it, and 'projection onto other'. So my childhood unhappiness and, at times, what I remember as being deep, deep despair; feelings of complete worthlessness and pointlessness at continuing to live, but not knowing how to get out of that prison sentence called life, being alive. I lived much of my life feeling trapped by life, tricked into being alive, punished by the ego and body's will to survive. Punished, because life had few moments of respite for me growing up and mostly I was constantly punished but rarely knew what about. Just for being me, the child they didn't want any more.

Those feelings were there though, and they taught me many wonderful things that I came to appreciate more fully later on.

And I clearly did survive.

I learned how to stop acting and instead learned how to write down everything I had understood along that journey from despair in childhood to happiness in later adulthood.

It started with attempts at fiction - but that didn't work for me, then poetry, some worked but others were awful, then my first raft of books which were third party concealed biography in many ways, and finally into memoir. That story is threaded through all these chapters; it is the story of my journey - Travelling the Alphabet Emotionally.

Depression is a combination of experiences, biology and mindset. Actually it is probably more complicated than that, but these are the three dimensions I used to work on for myself and the healing process.

Experiences – these can and do contribute to both the other two dimensions but can also be healed separately.

My experiences were dark and filled with terror at worst and anxiety at best. Oases of peace occurred but mostly when alone with nature. I acted like I was OK but could only manage that by freezing everything emotionally, being so closed down that nothing showed externally if I could help it.

Biology is the structure and wiring of your nervous system, how wired it is towards noticing the negative and not trusting the positive. Mine was utterly developmentally wired that way, again concealed behind a personality that was not who I am in my core, a brash out-there personality – which ADHD ably assisted and abetted- so my acting career was highly successful in its own way.

Mindset is how you interpret those experiences. Is it all about you? This is how a child thinks. I was certainly made to feel that too. Or is it just other people behaving badly- which it was, and is, mostly.

But mindset also allows you to change darkness into opportunity, into wisdom experiences and learning, to insight and enlightenment, distrustfulness into the most rewarding love I would have ever imagined, for my husband, my children and close friends but actually for everyone I have ever known too.

That surprised me greatly but once I saw it there inside me, I knew I could not ignore that either any more – when fear subsides, and the darkness goes, all that is left is love.

These three depression components interact but that was how I saw it for my own personal approach to change this into the gift that it ultimately became.

Baby and childhood experiences deeply affected my developing nervous system and created one that was hyper sensitive to any risk of danger or threat. Life after that just confirmed this reality constantly of course, in a self confirmation bias, for another three to four decades.

This means that my nervous system is still hardwired for anxiety and threat more than it is for peacefulness and stability, but I am slowly rewiring it using mindfulness. The other way that mindfulness practice works to soothe the causes and outcomes of depression is to help me reframe those experiences away from helplessness and victimhood to one of agency and self compassion, of responsibility and healing. That is a constant see-saw of effort but again it is working and more or less I do not feel a victim nowadays. Finally, the mindset of mindfulness approaches life as an adventure, a journey through all of its offerings, a nonjudgmental approach to experiences which finds much of value in all of them, especially the uncomfortable ones.

There are still the odd moments when I feel the futility of life weighing so heavily on me.

My garden, which you will meet elsewhere, and nature generally, have been my source of sanctuary for so many years since childhood, and now my second marriage is my haven of peace upon which I depend greatly.

I feel so blessed to have known dark times.

I can reassure people that the way out is there if you look for it

With the right mindset, work to soothe your biology and change it, using the amazing potential of neuro-plasticity and embrace it all as an experience – as part of a rich life filled with experiences.

And I tell you what – you never take anything wonderful for granted, even tiny things – once you have known darkness you appreciate every little scrap of light.

Equality, Fairness and Justice

Growing up I recall how strong my sense of justice, right, and wrong was. The basic instinct of fairness and in- equality is present in most young children in rather stark outline, until it becomes an understanding honed with experience and reflection.

Nowadays I still feel the same passion and fire for justice and equality but have learned how complicated that issue is; what seems like justice for one can seem very unfair to another.

Equality is the goal that we should all strive for in life. My sense of how important this is for everyone came from my experiences growing up when there was blatant inequality in our family.

There were hierarchies everywhere, favourites, those singled out for praise and those for denigration, or to be the scapegoat.

Such inequalities distorted all the relationships and left them vulnerable for breakdown in the future, which of course most did.

Inequality is an attitude, or a judgement wholly based on dualistic thinking and perceptions, good/bad, right/wrong etc. It is all based on an illusion that is both immediately harmful and divisive but also can create serious long-term damage to both individuals and the whole planet.

We, and everything else that exists, are all equally necessary as component parts of the whole of life and everything. Without one single part being present it is not complete or whole, that is why nothing is ever destroyed or created, it is just transformed from one set of molecules and energy to another grouping or format.

Creating hierarchies within the whole oneness is missing the point of oneness, but hierarchies are the basis of inequality.

Even hierarchies of sentience are becoming questioned in terms of what is sentience and how can it be measured.

For many centuries humans assumed they were the only sentient beings and white people assumed this only applied to white skinned people, hence the propensity for trying out surgical procedures on black slaves without any anesthetic and writing their screams off as a reflex action. We are now discovering not just sentience but levels of intelligence we never imagined before in all sorts of living beings that we never thought possible, most forms of animal life but also trees which communicate with each other over time and at speeds which mean we do not necessarily recognise it, because we're so species centric and blinded by that perceptual position.

What else might we discover that puts our arrogance into perspective in the future?

Keep an open mind please!

Equality can be a perception or a reality. For instance, the very real lived experiences of those in slavery, whether present day or historical, is a very real experience of denial of humanity and disempowerment based on a total absence of any equal consideration given to them as those imposing their condition would expect for themselves. It is a mindset of exploitation and inequality, of absence of respect and compassion.

One part of me is horrified that this is still true in modern times and that we have learned nothing from history, and another part of me understands that this comes from an experience where those soulless inhumane people are just individuals who have not been socialised or taught to hold all livings beings, human animal, plant, or mineral, in equal respect and veneration.

This single attitude shift would change everything overnight. It would end all forms of discrimination, abuse, exploitation, destruction, crime, unhappiness.

It would enable everyone to live co-operatively and supportively, no-one wanting more than they actually needed, no-one wanting somebody to suffer so they can have a larger share. It is the hunger of the empty human who seeks to consume ever more in order to feed their hunger, but they are never sated because the answer is inside them, in their deepest tender places and they won't look there.

So other people literally go hungry to feed their endless need for more, but that is an addiction this will never be sated, and we need to have compassion for them too. If this conversation could be explored openly, everywhere, it might make it more difficult for those hungry ghosts to continue as they do

Equality means power sharing, which is where it sometimes turns into a struggle. And we are all different in life, so some people want or cope well with power and some are just not bothered.

Power brings with it responsibility but it is equally open to abuses. Those who seek power are those most likely to also abuse it, as has been shown repeatedly throughout human history, especially political power because that brings with it power over so much else, including the law and resources.

Human society works best when we self-impose restrictions that prevent any individual having too much power or freedom to do as they want. It is the 'what they want' as opposed to 'what they need' that is the problem. Wanting so easily becomes a bottomless pit of more, more, more, at any expense, and that will mean less, less, less, for most other people and also habitat destruction, and speciesism, as we can also see throughout history of humankind.

Too much power leads to corruption so quickly, most of which is easily concealed through certain types of logical reasoning which omit the human responsibility or morality dimensions.

Mostly this is not even recognised, because that is too much responsibility. Big business has persuaded successive governments that they need de - regulation and de - restricting in order to run a healthy economy.

And yet instead of a healthy economy where everyone benefits, we see increasing exploitation, insecurity and human rights infringements for those who are not the ones wielding this power.

Humans need to have their power controlled by the greater masses to stop this perversion of potential occurring. We need to collectively police the individual and everyone should take part in that responsibility, but they don't want to.

Equality is utopian but not impossible. It is a matter of education. Humans are encouraged to be self serving survivalists and to see other humans as competition instead of co-operative support systems. Yet human survival on the planet in our early years only occurred because we used co-operative strategies to outwit the enormous odds stacked against us as a species. The 'other humans as competition' paradigm leads to fighting over resources in both global scales and also familial levels too. Yet there is actually enough for all if we just learn to work co-operatively.

There is no need to hoard if we all agree to care for each other collaboratively, we don't need rainy day savings because someone else will take care of us on the rainy day when we are too weak or old or sick to make our own contributions. We will already have earned that response from others by giving our all previously.

Equality for me is a passion because I can actually feel the suffering energy in the world as much as I can feel the joy and wonder of it all. It is a deep sadness because we all miss out so much on the beauty of life and human potentials by creating these false hierarchies.

And we hurt our own kind in the longer term too, we hurt them badly.

Our descendents, our grandchildren will look back on us and shake their heads in wonderment that we were so blind not to see how simple equality is, how liberating and loving and supportive and enriching.

If you asked me whether I wanted to be richer or for more people to have a better share - I would choose the latter, which is why some of my books are also fund raisers for those suffering inequalities the most.

Please if you read this - just think about how equality could improve your life and all those around you, and please do a little thing that makes it more likely to become a reality too.

Think how happy that would make you too. Because my early experiences of being at the bottom of the heap weren't very nice, and now I am closer to the top I can't stop thinking about how the others still down there are feeling, right now. You never forget.

Expectations and (pre)judgments

An expectation is a judgment in advance, a pre-judgment, a prejudice. It evolves from conditioned thinking processes that prevent us seeing what is actually there. We all do it, mostly unconsciously. It includes assumptions and (gender/race) role identities.

'I expect this of you, and if you do not meet my expectations then you have let me down'.

OR

'I expect this of you, and no matter what you actually do I will only see what I expected anyway.'

The potential for that to be the story is too great to risk because expectations are immediately impacted with the burden of 'fear of judgement'. 'What will you do if I don't live up to your expectations?' 'When will you see who I really am?'

It is all about the observer and has little or nothing to do with the person being expected of, 'the observed'.

My response to this is 'find out who I am first before you start placing these huge burdens on my shoulders which I may or may not be able to meet but are nothing to do with me'.

'Whatever expectations you have of me, be assured you will be disappointed.'

'Whatever your judgements of me, be assured they are probably mistaken.'

When I first met my wonderful David, this was one of the first things we said to each other, 'no expectations no agendas, let us find out who we each are'.

It worked!

Travelling the Alphabet Emotionally

Twenty plus years on, at the point of writing, we are still enjoying finding out who we each are and enjoying how much that changes over time. We come to each other heart, and eyes wide open, and mind willing to notice who we each are today, and not to stay resting in a place of non-seeing expectation and routine. Nothing about our life is truly routine although some of these exist for the sake of convenience and team work.

I am still finding out who David my husband is because he is still growing: creatively, musically, spiritually, emotionally, intellectually, even thought processes and sense of humour.

After all these years he continues to be very interesting to live with because he is endlessly evolving, and I still keep my mind open to whom he is becoming in each moment.

He meets my needs, emotionally etc. because he also allows me to grow and develop and become who I am. We are each other's voyage of discovery, 'chums' in that adventure, supports when the going gets tougher, mirrors for self-reflection when we need to re-evaluate. None of this is possible with expectations. They cloud up that mirror and prevent us seeing each other as we truly are.

The statement opposite is one I would like to have printed on a t-shirt, to be worn at all times when in any public situation. I have only ever experienced expectations as a burden which swamped me with their weight rather than allowing me to rise and show who I really am or what I can express of myself.

I also remember my son going on about how the teachers at school were all putting pressure on him to meet their expectations which they outlined very clearly – but none of them ever bothered to find out what he was really good at or how he could be helped to engage at school.

We didn't know the full picture at the time, but he had ADHD, dyslexia, and dyspraxia.

No wonder school was an impossible torture for him on a daily basis, as it is for so many children who do not fit the very narrow parameters of 'normal'- whatever that really means.

Normal is a brutal judgment too of course, the very concept excludes so many people. But it is the basis for so many expectations. 'It's only normal', 'that is not normal', who hasn't heard or even said that. Expectations are often seen as positive attitudes to hold which 'encourage others to shine'. It does the opposite. Your expectations of me are _your_ expectations, they may have nothing to do with what I can offer you. They are projections and thus potentially harmful, closing people down and placing pressure on them to meet your demands, needs and expectations.

Many relationships have failed on the back of expectations

An expectation is really an unspoken demand placed on someone without them even knowing about what the expectation really is. The energy taken up in coping with this means they are thus depleted. If you expect less from someone, they will likely expect less from themselves too, but they may just surprise you if you can see it, although the chances are that your lesser expectations will be all that you see.

But if you expect too much then you place that burden of anticipated failure in its place. The option to just be open to who someone is and to let them show you what they are capable of is the central point of balance and thus the right place to stand in your relation to others. This has been shown in schools where children, who are deemed not worth much, fail to even achieve their limited potential because that was not valued enough. Alternatively, children who are placed under too much pressure to perform can burn out and peak too young and end up failing to get to the next level of expected achievement.

I have seen both in my years teaching and realise the damage done by both.

**EXPECTATIONS are designed to MEET OTHER PEOPLES NEEDS,
not the needs of the individual to evolve into their full potential.**

I remember my time working as a school counsellor for three years and I asked a whole year 5 who they worked for at school. The answers that came back varied but were all incorrect. They said the teachers, parents, headmistress, even the government. They never said their own selves, their future selves, and the shock of realisation that went through the group when I pointed this out was tangible as a few dozen young minds suddenly understood the point of it all.

These children had all these burdens of expectation placed on them and had no understanding of their own part in it other than to please adults and get praise, both of which are very dangerous motivators. These are the two attributes that sexual groomers use. If a child knows the intrinsic value to themselves, they are free of the expectations of others since they are irrelevant.

Judgments are what occurs when the expectations are not met, and the disappointment sets in, or they over elevate the importance of someone and pedestals them so that they can never feel allowed to be human and fallible without that fall feeling like failure. They act like a form of gradual disillusionment and withdrawal – 'you are not what I thought you were', 'you're not who I want to be with'.

I challenge those thoughts with this alternative: -

How do you know that?

You haven't even bothered to look.

All you saw was your own self projected onto the other through your expectations, hopes, and desperate needs in some cases. It is such a tragic waste of potential on all sides and leads to so many 'groundhog days' for so many people.

I have been guilty of this and I have been on the receiving end too. Neither place is positive, or happy, or leads to lasting and fulfilling relationships. Recognising how damaging expectations are in any direction, i.e. higher or lower, is crucial to starting to reach that point of balance and openness that all people deserve.

When I meet someone who challenges me with their behaviour I find it helpful to seek out someone else who has a similar experience with that individual, and to share that until I can understand, accept it and embrace it.

The next time I see that person I am usually feeling very warm towards them because the understanding that the shared non-judgmental discussion has given me has enabled me to step back from the judgment that wants to stand between us. Reducing expectations to zero allows you to feel more comfortable with other people as well as for them to feel more comfortable with you.

I have to pick my confidantes well though, as it can easily be mis-judged as a slagging match, which it most certainly isn't because the motivation is to understand, not to judge or criticise.

Sometimes my being very literal has its advantages and sometimes it has its disadvantages.

Gradually though one collects a group of travelling companions who can understand that process with you, who have shared paradigms of 'understanding rather than slating', and with whom you can explore these relational complexities, without doing any harm to self or others.

So don't lower your expectations, remove them completely and instead be open to what people bring with them. It brings to mind the very well-known Rumi poem.

The Guest House

This being human is a guest house.

Every morning a new arrival.

A joy, a depression, a meanness,

some momentary awareness comes

as an unexpected visitor.

Welcome and entertain them all!

Even if they are a crowd of sorrows,

who violently sweep your house

empty of its furniture,

still, treat each guest honorably.

He may be clearing you out

for some new delight.

The dark thought, the shame, the malice.

meet them at the door laughing and invite them in.

Be grateful for whatever comes.

because each has been sent

as a guide from beyond.

Expectations and judgments only make you unhappy or dissatisfied with life, so do yourself a favour and let them go, move to openness and see what happens.
You never know who you might meet instead.

Food, and Fasting

Food is well known as a substitute for many other things in life, love being the most important. That can be love of self or love from others. My relationship with food has been both varied and transformative. Food is also an important part of travelling and often features as a highlight in some journeys but I have mostly dealt with that aspect in the destinations concerned

When I was growing up, we were as well fed as anyone was in those days of general lack that lingered after the Second World War, even though I was born ten years later. Food then was very basic and there were not that many programmes on TV that stimulated interest in cooking as an expression of anything at all. Food was all about need and function.

Except that my friend down the road was allowed cream soda to drink, I never was. I felt deprived. When I asked mum she just used 'not enough money' as the reason. It was always 'not enough' in our house hold, a very damaging attitude to live with. We were actually fairly middle class so 'not enough' was very relative and not real.

This lack attitude is a damaging one to live with when it is so clearly not true. It creates constant insecurity.

I was skinny as a girl, and I was often hungry, but I was well fed. For all her struggles with family life and parenting, my mother did do her best to feed us nutritionally and well, with a roughly weekly cycle of varied meals. I didn't like some of what she cooked but in retrospect it was good enough although now I would think it was bland.

I did eat as well as I was allowed.

It was the treats that we were deprived of; there were plenty of carbs but few in treat forms.

Again, in retrospect I think that was probably a good thing for me but at the time it simply added to the sense that there was no joy or sweetness allowed in our family, whether in relationship to each other or in what we had to eat.

I started secret eating when I was about nine or ten. I discovered a tin of Bournvita first and found that if I just took a couple of teaspoons of it at a time, no one seemed to notice it was being eaten down. I would let the crystals dissolve in my mouth and savour the forbidden sweetness and chocolate.

There was always chocolate in the house but it was always for mother and not for us. Rarely we were also allowed a piece or two whilst they were eating a piece or two most evenings. Again the overriding message was 'not for you'. Thus, treat food became a sort of 'punishment of withholding' which paralleled with punishment by withholding love or acceptance and all the other emotional needs children have when growing up.

Then I found I could sneak food when I went babysitting or to a friend's house. Contraband food tasted soooo much better and somehow fed my need to be able to survive under the radar.

I was given my school lunch money and chose to spend it on my own out of school choices rather than official lunches, sometimes not eating at all to spend it on music or books. Gradually over eating started to creep in and alternating between not eating and bingeing.

Then I started to gain weight, the bingeing always overtook the fasting, and I gradually more consciously hated my body even more than I already unconsciously had. It was the body that my parents found so despicable, so why should I have any appreciation of it either.

I started making myself vomit and taking large doses of laxatives.

I struggled for about two years and even got as far as trying to scrape the skin off my body with pumice stone to change how my body felt on the inside. I was frequently covered in tiny pin prick scabs and abrasions where I scrubbed harder.

It kind of gave me a slight high too, relieved some of the internal pressure of feeling so despicable that I constantly lived with. I now understand how that is a release of endorphins, which is why this kind of practice becomes so compulsive and addictive.

This could have continued and grown gradually more serious, but something stopped it just in time.

One day, I was about to resume my secret activities, when I heard a voice. Not my mind, that was too stuck in these routines I had created for myself. This voice seemed to be both inside and outside my 'self' and it said:

'you don't need to do this to yourself any-more.'

The emphasis was 'me' and 'myself'. I had taken over hurting me in between my parent's bouts. Just that, simple and profound! I hadn't realised I was doing anything specific, just things, habits, sneaky behaviours that had developed into ways to get my needs met. I wasn't even really fully conscious that I was doing half this stuff, it was like a dream flow, an unconscious series that went from one thing to another on a long and slippery slope downhill.

So what was it! That stopped me. That voice. That is another topic for discussion. But I heard it and did my best to stop. It took some effort and self-awareness but eventually I stopped the worst of it at least.

My weight stabilised again and I started to feel better about food.

I still would suddenly 'see food' that belonged elsewhere and feel the desperate need to steal some of it, though I did not see it as stealing, just taking a rightful share of that which had been withheld from me.

Around these times I took a couple of intended overdoses too, so clearly deeply disturbed. Again, another topic.

Eventually I got to eating mostly normally and being by now a married young woman I was in charge of food, so these anxieties died away. I was able to buy, cook and organise food so I could feel secure that my needs would be met. I also developed a passion for growing food and acquired an allotment which I managed organically. This need to 'produce' my own food has stayed with me and still does. Again, it put me in control of the means of my own survival.

More or less I continued to eat well, but I did experience occasional cravings for so called forbidden foods or treat foods, not always sweet things but fattening things more likely, such as bacon and cheese on toast with fried egg on top. I enjoyed being pregnant and breastfeeding as it more or less gave me free reign to indulge my food cravings and not put any weight on.

It was stopping feeding my sons when I had to take care. I could not allow myself to put weight on, that part of the body dysmorphia was still very strong. That would make me unpalatable to myself again and now I had lost the ability of my body to sustain others, it was all back to me and my lack of worth.

When my first marriage broke up, I was even more in control and that is when I started fasting too. I just spent some days not eating at all or not eating very much, keeping it to a minimum. It made me feel better, brighter in my brain, more energy. It also helped me keep very slim, which pampered the Dysmorphia further.

I found I enjoyed fasting; I enjoyed the challenge to my body of making it hungry and not giving into it. I think it was another slight form of body punishment/self-hatred, but it had positive outcomes and I could eat what I wanted most of the time too.

This was when I was single. It was almost a pride issue that I stayed thin without apparently trying.

When I was in relationships I rarely fasted since mostly I ate to match those around me, but I was careful to eat healthily and still very on top of dietary good health indicators. I see this as the positive indicators of my internal shifts in relation to food. But I struggled more with keeping thin, except that relationships always kept me slightly anxious and on edge, I never trusted anybody in those days, and that seemed to help me stay skinny although it did put a lot or pressure on my adrenalin system. I was terrified of the person I was in a relationship with finding out how worthless I really was. That never left me for a minute, and food was my comforter against that.

When I met David, I stopped fasting and we both ate heartily. We had taken on a massive derelict house project to set up our retreat centre. The sheer physicality of the work here made sure we used up any fuel we consumed. But I also started to actually trust, in small steps, to relax into a forever relationship as much as forever can possibly exist, which of course it doesn't, but again that is another debate.

Menopause came and for the first time in my life I started to gain weight in ways I had never even had to think of before. Also, during this time, I was very ill, and everything changed. My weight gradually went up and up, not massively at all, but heavy by my standards.

Fasting became fashionable and we agreed to do it together; David and I. To start with it was hard. I had problems with blood sugar highs and lows and am well aware that both my parents and younger brother are diabetics of one sort of another. The first few times it was challenging. I developed headaches, swooning, nausea, and dizziness. But I stuck with it and got through these side effects until they died away.

Around this time, I also started going on retreats regularly and this rekindled my fear of not being in charge and thus not getting enough food. I found myself over eating just to make sure, until I was able to recognise for the first time how important my issue of being in control of the food supply had been over the years.

We are asked not to be greedy on retreat, to consider others needs and I never felt I was being greedy, but I needed to get my fair share of food because the inner child never got any share of the love available and that was sparse enough at the best of times. Once I was able to recognise that cause of craving and dissolve it, I was fine and even fast occasionally on retreats too nowadays.

As I write this I realise I enjoy fasting and eating equally; feeling hunger as just a physical sensation and I have deep gratitude that it is not a life sentence as it is for so many. Fasting makes me more aware of the suffering caused by hunger, makes me more grateful for the food that I have available to me, makes me love growing and preparing my own food on a seasonal basis.

I still have food insecurity, even though my life is filled with love. My back has collapsed badly now, and I can no longer garden much at all. I can only grow some of my own fruit and vegetables.

We have to move from a home with land to a house with an easily managed plot, and that is proving deeply emotionally challenging yet again. It is clear I still have more layers to uncover and let go of concerning my relationship with food. Can I still grow my needs? But fasting has been so helpful.

I have also recognised with the house/ garden move, that I have resorted to secret and rebellious forms of eating as comfort once more, a deeply maladaptive coping strategy for such stress.

Then I am fasting to remove any weight gained but once more as a form of punishment. So that tendency is still deeply rooted within my unconscious. I still have more work to do in this healing area.

I will continue to fast whenever my body feels the need for it, and to use it to cleanse my mind and body of those attachments and defilements. I use it as a part of my mindfulness practice, not to be caught up in the whims of the body and mind but to act consciously at all times as much as I am able to. I am now able to be more discerning about what I eat and am noticing how certain foods make my body feel, more or less clogged up or clean, sluggish or alert. It is still an interesting journey with food through my life. I am no longer interested in competitive cooking for friends or skills development, but I move further towards foraging and wild food too, preserving through fermentation. The journey continues but in different directions nowadays.

Forgiveness

In a spiritually soul-searching approach to life, I have sought to find an ever deeper understanding of those experiences, and what it all means on the spiritual level. In these 'Alphabet' essays I have found three topics that stand out for study more than any others, those of forgiveness, compassion and gratitude. From my experience I have found that these skills draw together all the other learning and, along with a good dose of humility and openness, they allow us to express our best version of 'self' possible.

They are familiar words and most people assume they understand what the word means but in practice how easy are they to fully master and not to masquerade as something else, such as denial or suppression or even cognitive dissonance, and attribution bias, where we change stories to fit our own perception of self, or where we blame circumstances around us for dimensions of who we also are which we self- judge as not being acceptable.

So how do we fully learn to understand and recognise these attributes of deeper spiritual growth and also fully develop them as a skill set within ourselves, since knowledge without deep application is of little or no value at all?

Forgiveness is one of those skills that I, like many, found particularly hard to achieve.

I understood that forgiveness was something that benefitted me more than those I forgave and I'm not a particularly vindictive kind of person, so harbouring grudges is not really my thing either. But forgiveness is also not feeling angry any more. That part was / is harder.

I had rigorously trained myself to understand and accept that forgiveness does not mean it was ok what happened, or that you are also asked to forget what happened to you.

But could I feel forgiveness also?

Like most humans, not immediately.

I also accepted and worked hard at turning all my abusive experiences into positives for me and my life as it evolved over time. But even though I had read and recognise forgiveness as an end your own feelings of anger, I felt that there was still more to it. This writing project is a huge part of that process too.

Fear of it happening again makes you defensive. That can appear to others to be anger, so you can appear angry and not really feel angry, just afraid that you are going to be damaged again. You have to understand the difference inside yourself to work with this dynamic; fear and anger are so closely linked.

For a long time, forgiveness still wasn't complete for me; I still felt afraid, still felt defensive. I also still felt angry that what had been done to me, had taken so much of my life and potential away, and left me with so much sh*t to clear up on my own. I still harboured resentment that this had happened to me, that I had borne the brunt of all that ignorance and unkindness.

Stories have been used throughout the world traditions to facilitate this understanding and self-recognition process. Stories as metaphors for life have always been a powerful influence on me and sometimes I can read them and they stay with me, even if they don't make complete sense at the time.

I have used them here in this book also.

One particular story that I read, so long ago I can't remember where I got it from, stayed with me in my unconscious mind. I think the Tibetan book of Living and Dying but this is a variation on the one printed there about Asanga waiting to meet Maitreya.

It could even be a fusion of stories that emerged as this one in my mind, which ever outcome it is, I clearly hadn't deeply understood it on first encounter, although I thought I did. Now I realise that was on an intellectual level only. However, it must have stayed inside my store mind waiting for a time when I would need its wisdom.

When it later returned to me in its entirety, during my recovery from my PTSD breakdown, it worked for me on a much deeper level and did the magic of transformation. It has shown me so many layers of meaning so I thought I would like to share it. It is that watering process which Thich Nhat Hanh talks of, when suddenly it is the right time for a particular seed to flourish fully. And so it was for me with this story. I share it with you in the hope that it can enlighten you also at some point.

The rotting dog.

A young monk was asked by his master to walk to the nearby town and collect some provisions. He walks along the road, mindfully enjoying time away from the temple, collects the errands and returns. The master asks him if he noticed anything as he walked along.

'No nothing master, I'm sorry was I supposed to look out for something.'
'No that is fine,' says the master.

A year later the young monk is asked to make the same trip. This time he notices a dog lying by the side of the road, its body covered in sores and its wounds full of maggots. He stops and looks, then hurries on past concluding there is nothing he can do to help. He collects his packages and returns to the master, who repeats his question, 'Did you see anything along the road as you walked.'

'Yes, I did see an injured dog, but I left it there as there was nothing I could do to relieve its suffering. Should I have done differently?' 'No that is fine, says the master.

A year later the request and journey are repeated and when he sees the dog, is surprised it's still there. He carefully finds a feather to brush away the maggots, so he does not hurt them either, then lifts the stinking rotting dog across his shoulders to find someone in town who can help. When he arrives and asks people for help, they all laugh and talk to each other about the young monk with an imaginary dog. At the far end of the town he finds someone who agrees to help and gently takes the dog. He collects his packages and tells the master what happened. The master seems pleased with this news.

A year later all is repeated but this time he sees a frail little old man sitting cross legged and smiling broadly from ear to ear. He asks to be carried into town. The young monk carefully lifts the old man onto his back and carries him, even though it slows him down greatly. When they arrive the young man asks people to help him find shade for the old man but everyone gives him strange looks and avoids him, except one man who says, 'I can't see an old man on your back but why are you carrying around that rotting dog, it looks like it would be better being put to death.'

The young man is astonished that no one can see this old man whose weight he feels strongly, but he searches around until he finds someone who offers to help the old man, then he goes to collect his packages.

On returning to the monastery he tells the master who chuckles with great joy and is clearly very pleased to hear this story. 'What does this mean master' the young man asks.

The master says simply, 'One can only perceive that which the mind is open to.

One is often too blinded by ignorance to notice what can be done to help others and see that of Buddha/ God/good in everything, to see their true nature.'

****

What a story really; repetitive and nothing much happens except that slight evolution of consciousness as each year goes by. That is what forgiveness really takes, a gradual understanding, a gradual recognition of responsibility to, and for, self and others.

I forgot clean about that story until the moment I was completely ready for its fullness to be revealed to me. When it came back it was like all the lights on and fanfares ringing out at once.

Now I use it to constantly remind myself of how to maintain compassionate thoughts and feelings towards people where once I might have held judgment and separation/ withdrawal. Now I can see myself along that same journey and acknowledge times when I was just too hurrying to get through things to really see what was there and now I rejoice that I do see what is there most of the time, that of the Buddha in everything.

Sometimes people hurt us badly and are quite unable to recognise their action as unkind; they have not yet understood. How easily we fail to see what need there is in the world. We are so busy running our own errands that we are unable to open our minds beyond, to truly perceive what else is present and how we might choose to respond.

Another slightly different version of this phenomenon which I came across was a legal term called 'willful blindness', when we choose not to see because if we actually pay attention and notice something actively, then we might have to take action.

So we pretend not to see, it's easier that way, and we can salve our conscience by saying it's not our problem. And we can walk on by, as so many did in my life and then later said they hadn't realised. And I wonder how many times I have also done exactly this.

This attitude of mind occurs within all areas of life but also there are people who are humble enough to accept being further educated, to be asked to re-think their opinions and to consider that they might be mistaken. Of course there are some who are too convinced of their rightness too. Again to learn this lesson fully, I have to admit I have been both.

As someone who has explored most of the spiritual traditions, I have struggled to understand the Christian teachings on forgiveness. As they were given to me as a child, they didn't make sense. How many times should I forgive someone and let them abuse me again? Seventy seven? So many.

Could I survive that?

What happens after 77, what if it went to 80 etc. I was too hurt, angry, terrified to consider forgiveness, but I was awestruck with Jesus example. Even whilst dying on the cross, Jesus said 'forgive them; they do not know what they do'.

The rotting dog story gave me that answer combined with the explanation of willful blindness. And thus, instead of adding even more layers of anger to my story I was able to recognise that I too was guilty of this behaviour and therefore could not judge or stay angry. With that my anger melted and I found forgiveness rested in its place.

So what about this issue of ignorance, blindness, lack of perception or lack of self-reflexiveness? With sufficient honesty and understanding of the interconnectedness of everything, let us consider how it affects us all and in so many ways.

Well first of all forgiveness comes from a place of deep understanding of the limited perceptual abilities of each person, as exemplified in the Rotting Dog story. There is no point in expecting people to do things or to understand things that are just far beyond their open-mindedness or emotional awareness and thinking capacity. Judging them on the basis of our own expectations and abilities is a pointless exercise in self-satisfied, self-justification; we can all fall into that trap. Even when we try not to, we do; we all make those micro-judgements without knowing the full story, without being prepared to truly work to understand the experience of the other.

People, you, me and everyone else, are all doing their best – no matter how limited that may be, and my own experience shows me how it can be frustratingly limited, but nevertheless it is their best, sometimes my best too.

These teachings of how the master treated his young student, of how those who chose to support the assassination of Jesus, and of so many other teachings of a similar nature, show how gently these students are to be dealt with, because forceful attempts to teach people how to open their perception can only fail.

Frustration with others for not seeing what we see, or want them to see, can make us angry, hurt, confused, and feel very isolated. It is easy to turn on those people as the source of that hurt. We may try harder; shout louder; demand; insist; bully; tease; reject and many other ways of trying to force the perceptual shift we want them to perceive. This is a closing down technique, not an opening, teaching technique, yet it is commonly used by many people, as if berating and shouting makes one's voice and message heard more clearly. It just doesn't. Shows of verbal violence and bullying is more about fear than learning and growing.

Quaker and Buddhist peace workers know this and work carefully to avoid it because it has the opposite effect to that desired for an effective outcome. I have seen it happening in school with young children being shouted at by teachers who presumed their charge should understand what they are being reprimanded about and I myself have both been on the giving and the receiving end of this approach. Now I have learned how not to get my message across, I too am learning better ways to get heard gently and legitimately by those who are open to new ideas.

Sometimes we do have to say 'No', though. Sometimes we have to say 'enough', or 'I can't do this anymore', because we can risk colluding with people who are stuck in their own patterns of damaged and damaging behaviour. We are entitled to walk away but to do so with love and forgiveness and not anger or resentment. We do have our own life to live also.

Mental health has been brought into the political and social limelight a little more recently. I believe that the perception of such issues could do with a little help in understanding and forgiveness, which would deepen compassion within families and communities everywhere. I have had the experience of two sorts of mental health problem; post-traumatic stress disorder (PTSD) and resulting depression, I also have a cognitive disorder better known as ADHD, though I am more ADD.

The first is a sense of permanent terror which has no basis in present reality and is caused by a complete overloading of the individual's nervous system' ability to cope with stress, especially the kind of stress that deeply threatens a sense of personal integrity, safety and worth.

Service people are particularly prone to PTSD because their lives are at risk and they are expected to take action which can kill other humans and cause widespread destruction.

Travelling the Alphabet Emotionally

I believe when the commandment not to kill was given it was not just because it was bad for the person being killed, but because it is an action that you cannot take back and the consequences are damaging to the killers' sense of integrity as a fellow human. This is why all war must be wrong, because people are asked to do things that may destroy their own humanity. The international development of forgiveness would likely put an immediate end to all war.

Resilience is seen as a bulwark against such conditions developing, but the risk is that resilience may be seen when it is more a lack of humanity that is present, a lack of empathy and compassion, which both Jesus and Buddha taught were the most important aspects of being human. The ability to keep coping with inhuman expectations and demands placed upon you.

Much PTSD is now also recognised as coming from childhood abuse, and other life shocking events such as rape and assault. It can dramatically distort the still developing child's brain in early years and especially the areas concerned with stress and emotional processing, making these areas dominant and over-sensitized.

I tried many forms of help and finally found mindfulness suited me and was able to recognise the PTSD as distinct from me as a person, i.e. when it kicked in and what triggered it and how I could manage it.

I also found there was something else which only became visible once the PTSD symptoms diminished, but which still seemed to be triggered by the same kind of echoes of my childhood agendas of abuse.

I gradually shut my life down and retreated further and further to avoid these triggers but I realised I was living in fear of being triggered and that my quality of life was becoming more and more restricted, including attending my local Sangha and Quaker meeting since triggers had come from there too.

But it seemed that nowhere was safe except my immediate family i.e. my husband, sons and very close friends with whom I'd shared my life story and who could relate to my experiences. I spent a part of my life hiding from having my second arm cut off in other words, but I also knew that the people who had triggered my illness did not mean it and that if I was normal i.e., without these shadows in my life, then I would merely be miffed and be able to shrug it off. There was always something not quite right about what happened to trigger me, but my reaction was extreme, so I knew that the problem was mine to deal with. Avoiding having my second arm cut off metaphorically was ruining my life and stopping me from healing.

I did not want to be a victim to these triggers, but I did not know how to deal with them. So many people kept saying 'just put the past behind you' without realising how impossible that still was for me. They assumed that I either had not tried to do just this or that I did not want to, that I reveled in my damaged status. None of these assumptions were true. I had sought every kind of therapy and intervention I could find, within and outside the NHS. I had even trained in several myself in a hope of 'Physician heal thyself' being the outcome alongside wanting to help others on a similar journey to mine.

Nothing thus far had completely worked. I now understand this is the difference between traumatic recall and bad memories, the former just do not get processed and healed over time like other memories can do, even unhappy ones. How many of you are still haunted by your first partner rejection for instance, or your first failure at something. Those memories matter less and less as time goes by, but trauma is stuck in exactly the place where it happened and it does not move from there without a great deal of effort and skill. Trauma takes specific willingness to let go of and usually takes some time and iterations.

But then one afternoon just before Christmas I was sitting down idly watching a film on TV whilst frantically knitting a jumper I wanted finished before Christmas. The film was one in the Harry Potter series, in which ghoulish creatures called Dementers make a significant appearance as captors and torturers of the worst kind. Their method of torture was to suck every last thought, feeling and memory of anything good that every happened in your whole life out of you, and to leave you with no hope. This was a completely accurate description of what happened to me when triggered, that same feeling of dark, bleak desolation that engulfed me was being described and illustrated on the film. It was so accurate I was shocked, then realise that JK Rowling had also suffered periods of depression herself and had used this to describe those creatures. I felt such empathy for her in that moment, and for all people who have depression and PTSD. I had come a long way by this time.

But suddenly I felt a deep gratitude for the Dementers being in my life as they had shown themselves finally to me, instead of always haunting me in the shadows and curtailing so much. I had always felt that my mental illness was not me; that it was something that sat within me but was separate from me; it controlled me from within but wasn't my own nature; that it was not a judgement of me, not a measure of my personal worth and not an addiction, but I had never had a way of identifying it as this separate entity.

This story had just given me the clue. I could now laugh at Dementers as being nothing of substance, to know that they could never take anything from me that truly mattered; my husband and children had shown me that.

Most other family members had walked by unseeing, or even seen but still walked by.

Some had tried to help by telling me to put the past behind me and then judged me for not being able to do that, judged me for my desperation to feel safe and to be free, for living un-triggered.

In truth I had also in the end ranted at them and rejected them for their lack of understanding and desire for me to pull myself together and get over it, without them ever having to look at themselves. They weren't ready to see any rotting dogs and they resented me for showing it to them. Now, for me, that is completely OK, and I totally get that, I understand, I have done similar elsewhere, they are just fallible humans and I forgive them utterly. I do still get triggered but I treat it as an exercise in rewiring my nervous system, and gradually that is working.

We all only live with stories inside our heads all the time. Life is just one big story that we tell our self and we seek to confirm it or change it by finding the interpretation needed to be able to change the story. Sometimes reframing is just not enough if the story is too dark and haunting to respond to that approach. I had already identified the level of fear I lived with, through a wonderful Experiment with Light retreat at the Quaker retreat centre in Birmingham called Woodbrooke, but these Dementers gave me a practical image which I could then use to laugh at, to dispel, to deeply and fully recognise and understand, that I was afraid of fear itself, since it is fear that robs us of the Joy of Life. I had seen the film before and not recognised this description because I was not ready to see it at that point. I had not made enough of my own 'journeys to market' yet.

I tell my story because I hope it helps others to find their story, or to understand further how to help those who struggle with these burdens and recognise that there is that of good/ god/ Buddha in all things.

Travelling the Alphabet Emotionally

Once one has lived without joy or hope, one never takes it for granted and every moment, every breath has become my celebration of joy which is at the heart of what I believe both Jesus and Buddha tried to get us to see. But too many of us are still trying to get to market.

It takes time to make that journey, but first it takes a desire to start it, and to recognise that need for it within each one of us. And it takes forgiveness and compassion from those around us to wait while we each take it, if we and they can see the rotting dog at all.

Friendship

Can friendship be measured?

Is friendship measured by the time spent in vigil at my dying friends' bedside or is it rather found in the memories of shared laughter and love, of shared sorrows and the time spent quietly listening to each other in a life time of joys and woes?

Is friendship the relationship that truly transcends all others since there is no hereditary or legal obligation and it is truly a choice of free will to be close and to give your love to that other?

It is the friendship within a marriage that also keeps that love alive when passions are faded by time and familiarity, and coloured by stress and demands; it is the friendship that enables it to endure.

It is friendship that keeps siblings in close contact, shared memories again, and shared histories too. When siblings fall apart it is from lack of true friendship. It is when self-interest and historical conflicts take over because there is not enough friendship to succour the heart and keep the love alive and flourishing.

Spending time with other people is best when it is freely chosen and not out of obligation or a sense of duty. Anything given from free choice is by far the greater gift than anything given from duty, selfish need fulfilment or any manipulative basis of interaction. Friendship does not need to occur. We are not obliged to form friendships with other people, it is a free will choice, or it should be, at all times, if it is true friendship.

There should be no expectations, just an acceptance of all that the other can offer you in relationship. They are free to give their best when they are left to offer their gifts from choice.

There should be no demands, how can someone give you their best if you are too busy demanding it of them, and their gift is diminished greatly by demands, by pressure, by need fulfilment behaviours.

A true friendship can creep up on you and take you by surprise.

It can come from the most unlikely backgrounds.

It can develop between the most unlikely matches of people.

Sometimes friendships develop not from any superficial compatibility but from a deep heart connection, an unseen knowing of some deep hidden past, an energy of recognition from souls rather than any obvious social 'needs meeting' intentions.

When we can stand alone, on our own terms, then our friendships are free to develop as they would and without agendas. When we can look someone in the eye and say, 'I do not need you, but I choose to spend my time and share my gifts with you', what greater gift can you be given, a gift of freedom and affection, companionship, being there for each other. We all have such gifts to give to others.

Friends such as these are real treasures, truly precious offerings, bringing with them moments to honour and hold sacred.

When my close friend died today I realised the true nature of the gift she had been to my life. I will hold her memory sacred in honour of the life she shared with me. She showed me how to be a true friend. A wise teacher. A true gift.

This first piece was written in honour of Hilary Kearsley, my dear friend who passed away in august 2018- she was a quiet inspiration.

There is of course much more to say on the topic of friendship. I have other friends who are soulmates and who have 'been there' for me in just the right way at different times in my life.

And I have had friends who have clearly not been there for me at all but merely for themselves.

Sometimes a friendship develops where there is much to seem an obvious connection of shared interests and yet over time no depth develops, it continues at arm's length emotionally.

Narcissism / NPD also comes within friendships, with people who love bomb you and cannot do enough for you, who cannot receive equally and thus the friendship starts to feel more like a Buy-up full of conditions. Once you break those conditions either accidentally or because you are refusing to meet them, the story changes - dramatically sometimes.

I am not good at relationships kept at a distance. I tend to want to make emotional connections with people. For me personally it feels very superficial to maintain a supposed friendship with someone for whom you have no connection and although occasional good fun dinner parties are ok, they are empty and meaningless and not something I am any good at, at all.

Really close friends are people who you can see and not see for months on end and then pick up as if it were minutes instead of months. Really close friends are people who understand how you think and do not judge you for it, whilst being able to be honest about your shortcomings, and still accept you for who you actually are.

Friends can see beyond the surface and actually want to nurture that dimension hidden in plain sight.

Other people will not recognise that about you or may want to keep you in a certain place, so they know where you are, and their hierarchy is maintained.

You can tell by how they talk to you, the language they use, the attitudes they take when you mess up and want support.

I have a close friend who nearly died and was on life support for about six months. There were three of us who had worked together.

When my friend started to recover and made the decision to go back to her old job as head of Math's in large school, this other friend was so incensed that she would not take early retirement on health grounds immediately and thus remain 'ill' for the rest of her life.

Her colleagues likewise seemed more angry than pleased at her recovery and her acting replacement was most put out by her return to health.

She has now semi retired at the appropriate age, having shown that with determination you can come back even after life changing health issues. The other close 'friend' still does not speak to her however.

Some friendships are built on hierarchies of entertainment value or superiority value to the so-called friend- who is then put out when you evolve and move past them.

They were not true friends, just stages in your development of realising your own true worth. Sometimes two people can do the same thing to each other at the same time because they cannot communicate effectively about what is happening to them. Losing friends in this way is not necessarily a sign of your failure but maybe a sign of your progress. Once you have seen the Buddha or the rotting dog even, you cannot go back. And if those around are unable to see it with you, the connections between you are no longer in balance.

Some people measure their self worth by how many 'friends' they have. It is better to measure the depth of the friendships you do have, even if it is only one, than to keep a collection of meaningless numbers. People are not commodities and should be treasured at whatever level you are capable of. One of the biggest threats to our overall mental health is the lack of direct contact nowadays and the increasing online alternatives which stop people making those deeper connections that are so important for us as humans.

Friendship is a gift.

Nurture it, but make sure it is friendship and not something else.

If it allows you to be yourself fully that is friendship, even as you evolve.

If it is something that you can chuck away easily enough then it is not friendship at all and should not be considered as such.

Friendship can be a life saver too. New research has shown that our immune systems are far less effective when we are isolated and far better at protecting us when we are not socially excluded. It is thought to go back to early human when survival was utterly dependent on group living and harmony. Like hunger, loneliness can be a threat to life. So, develop and value those friendships as much as you can. They may just save your life.

Gratitude

Gratitude opens the heart to the joys of life and shrinks the stuff we don't enjoy into context, to merely the experience that taught us this or that, or whatever. Gratitude is my favourite mindfulness practice and I do it every day in some way or another. It threads through every moment of my life and weaves a net of gentleness around the harshness that would invade and diminish that life.

Thank you for this moment, thank you for this breath, thank you for consciousness that allows me to recognise the gift in this moment, in this breath.

Thank you for my childhood, it taught me the importance of self-awareness and conscious development; of a spiritual approach to life that includes compassion and awareness at its heart.

Thank you for my parents who were so damaged and misguided in their life together that they destroyed so much of their own happiness. A role model can provide an example of how **not** to be as much as how to be. You were both never grateful for the children you had, never grateful for what you shared in life and never grateful for all the blessings that came your way daily. You did not deeply understand gratitude, not the deepest sense of gratitude for simply everything. You gave me that gift because without your example I would not have gone searching for that understanding.

Thank you for my children. You taught me the true meaning of mental elasticity, stretching mine until it broke and when I repaired it, it was better, longer, stronger, again and again. Thank you for teaching me how totally forgiving love can be when it is free from agendas and selfishness.

Thank you for being my friends and seeing me as a human and not an archetype provider just for your needs.

Thank you for teaching me to love in the first instance, to unfreeze me from my protective frozen state of emotional prison. Only you two would ever have the power to chip that shell open enough for the rest of me to slowly emerge.

Thank you for my body. I put you through so much, body dysmorphia, bulimia, self-harm, comfort eating. And then all the illnesses and operations I went through. You stuck with it and now I honour you deeply although you are damaged and struggling to remind me to be more careful with you.

I am nowadays. I work with you and we are good friends. I honour all parts of you down to each toe and each hair follicle, each new flake of skin that grows each day to replace each old one that falls away. I honour your ability to renew and replenish me daily, to heal my ills and wounds.

I honour your teachings of the body/ mind connections, reminding me to meditate, to let go, to take exercise and enjoy my food, to avoid poisons that are seen as socially desirable, alcohol, sugar etc.

I honour your inner workings of blood, muscle, tissue, organ, keeping me conscious, breathing and experiencing the breath, the moment. You show me the joy of lying naked on my husband's naked body in the morning, just briefly lying there continuing that wonderful conversation between skin and skin of two people who love each other deeply, that last lingering intimate embrace before the day begins in earnest.

Thank you for my mind. It has led me on a merry dance of possibilities, of stories of how it is, and then helped me to recognise how internal narratives and fictions can hurt us and separate us from the true nature of living, of being alive in this moment.

Thank you for trying to protect me from perceived threats and the burdens that crushed me when I was younger, you froze and kept me safe until it was time to let it all out, and you chose that time well, when I had the love in my life to keep me alive through it. Then you let me remember it all and release it all.

Thank you for working with my heart, to let me wake up fully to the wonders of deep love and kindness that now surrounds me daily. It is all in the mind. How we open that mind is our daily challenge, our daily choice.

Thank you for a life of choices. It may not seem like it because we are not in control of the world, no matter how much power we think we wield. In each moment I choose to be grateful, open, happy, concerned, and awake. We always have that choice and ultimately it is the only choice that is necessary.

Thank you for my intelligence, my logical and rather literal brain, my alternatively wired brain that sees life differently to some others but is similar to a minority group. We illustrate the alternative realities that some people will deny exist. You helped me to find the answer to the great questions that hang in everyone mind – why? What is the point of it all? What is the truth? Who am I?

Thank you for the gift of emotions, energy in motion flowing through a body, through consciousness. Good or bad, hard or soft, you show me the tapestry of life, the loose edges and threads we can pull on to unwind areas and reweave their story. You show me the flow of life, the experience of each moment with joy and pain in equal measure, the one only existing because the other is there too.

Thank you for the gift of love, that wellspring of connection we have at heart level as much as we are able to open our hearts to.

My heart opened gradually as I allowed it to, or else when it was cracked open by mental illness and I lay exposed and vulnerable and learned not to fear this state of being, then I learned to love openly, all things, to love and accept but still be able to make choices, to discern the more skilful paths through life.

Love showed me its power in the face of unkindness; it lay there awaiting the invitation to re- emerge as I faintly remember feeling as a young child loving everything without judgement.

Thank you for mental illness and post-traumatic stress disorder. You showed me not to be afraid of being broken and vulnerable, how to truly care for myself emotionally, to trust my intuition about people and their energy, if they are full of the toxicity of anger and self-pity, to keep my distance and not get drawn back into those worlds. They are reminders and glimpses into the hell realms to keep me out.

Being broken open reveals who you really are, until the wound crusts over and the struggle to keep yourself open and alive continues, but being raw and opened like that, you never forget it, you never want to lose it, it is the holy grail of awareness and consciousness, you never want to rebuild those walls of defensiveness and protection, they are false friends who imprison you.

These experiences taught me deeper compassion for both myself and for others. There are knock-ons from this: less judgement, more kindness, less ignorance, more understanding, less tactlessness more sensitivity.

Everything about this time in my life has been great in the outcome but horrendous in the during.

Yet everything passes.

Time taught me that even if it takes a lot of my life time it is all always worth it. So many lessons to be grateful for, I cannot enumerate them all.

Travelling the Alphabet Emotionally

Thank you for my garden, for the flowers food and joy which all grow therein. I have loved working with and in you, being nurtured through the dark days by your gentle healing power of just being in the moment, always there, never judging or rejecting, just being exactly what you are. I love the flowers, they represent hope and colour and the future. They nurture all around them, food, growth, change, decay and death into rebirth, all this is represented in single flower if we look deeply enough.

I am grateful for the natural love, for all the unconditional love that so much around us shows for us just by being there, supporting our lives, the trees, the water, the flowers they all show their love for our wellbeing by their very presence on this planet. It is love in action. We cannot exist without them. The sun loves us every day just by existing and thus keeping us alive.

I have endless gratitude for the Dharma, and especially the ways in which it has been made accessible by contemporary writers and translators, most notably Thich Nhat Hanh. I have written more about this in its own book, but I cannot exclude it from my gratitude list.

Thank you for all the weather, the gentle puff of cooling air on a warm summer day, the raging torrent that reminds us how insignificant we are in the face of nature and we mess with her at our peril. For day and night, and all in between times, for stars in the sky and clouds that I can trace into my morning cup of tea.

I am grateful for those who do not like me or find me difficult to take to. They keep reminding me not to think I am anything special, that other people's perceptions of me are not about me, that I am not the centre of the universe. They remind me to stay humble and accepting of myself and other people. To stay open and not to allow myself to make judgments of those others in case I hurt them.

If I do not stay in gratitude for all things, I am diminished by the meanness of spirit that can take its place. If I let it slip and become resentful or craving, I feel myself becoming tighter and smaller and darker. My gratitude comes from my heart, it is not a mental activity; the mind is just the tool to express the joys of the heart.

Gratitude is what is possible when we are facing fears and dis-empowering them with humour, openness and love; it is the best way to free one's self. On the other hand, what do you replace the fears with, what do you want to replace them with? My answer to that is happiness, out of which grows confidence and all the other good stuff. This is the power of gratitude.

We spend far too much time focusing on what is wrong in life and never enough time focusing on what we already have. Taking anything in life for granted means that we push away the very things we yearn for, having deep gratitude for everything we already have which in turn makes us more attractive for 'the more' that we yearn for, that if it comes towards us, we will be truly and deeply appreciative of its arrival and presence in our life.

Gratitude builds happiness in bucket loads, which is what you use to fill the gaps left by your released and reduced fears. That is what stops them returning in another form. That is what turns the fears into wonderful lessons in 'how not to be' so you can do more of how to be in your life.

Gratitude is one of the most uplifting joys in life and, as a daily meditation, I would never want to be without it ever again.

Honesty.

Do you know Third Rock from the Sun, a US TV comedy show which ran for about 6 series and depicted four aliens arriving on earth to observe and report back on humankind's habits and relationships? In one episode Dick is faced with the vagaries of human communication, and in particular honesty.

The list that justifies each item of dishonesty being challenged goes like this, brutally frank, bending the truth, flattery, figure of speech, polite conversation, diplomacy. I love this episode. It spoke to me so deeply because I too struggle with these vagaries of social conversation and this summed it up for me completely.

All of it is dishonesty that has a socially acceptable face. Yet to be branded a liar is a deep insult and something most people want to avoid, and indeed invest a great deal of self-worth into not being dishonest. And yet is it possible to be honest in its complete sense? We can consciously work towards it, that is for sure, but honesty is one of those impossibly challenging things in life because it is not the normal form of human communication, whatever we want to argue. And in order to explore honesty, first of all we have to address the concept of truth, at what cost, and following that discussion, what then does honesty mean and to what level it is achievable?

What is truth? Well we can mostly all agree that there is never one single truth at human level and there is probably one truth that is above all else and which is unknowable by humans. We can be more confident of the former point because whatever we think is fact is usually later proven to be mistaken or incomplete or superseded, either scientifically or historically.

We each have our individual truth, our personal narrative of our life based on our own deepest experiences. There is nothing to say that anybody else will share that narrative- yet it can feel like it is absolute truth to us. If we are too foolish, we allow our ego to invest too much into that version of truth so that it becomes a prison. If, then, someone else has an opposing point of view of our narrative, is their truth right and ours wrong or are they all true depending on how you look at it?

If we can live with this dialectic then we can get along with others, but when we need to be absolutely right, *then* we will experience clashes and conflict with other people who cannot find it in their hearts to embrace this point of view either. They usually cannot even begin to listen to it, let alone consider it thoughtfully and perhaps acknowledge there is some truth in it.

Honesty is the first chapter in the book of wisdom – Thomas Jefferson

So, does honesty depend upon absolute or relative truth or is it something separate.

Let me get back to socially acceptable dishonesty.

Tact sums up most of the forms listed above from Third Rock. This feels a deeply dishonest form of lying because it is dressed up in good intentions and social acceptability – to many people it is the facilitator of smoothly running human interactions. But can we trust it?

The secret of life is honest and fair dealing – if you can fake that you've got it made – Groucho Marx.

I feel the energy of tact as patronising and confusing and it leaves me utterly not trusting or wanting to spend more time with that person.

Give me some one direct and honest and up front, even if what they say is hurtful, at least it is honest. If I get a whiff of tactfulness, my antenna goes up and my trust goes out of the window.

However, I come from a background where I was taught never to trust anything anyway.

When you are endlessly told 'the family don't like you they are only nice to you because they are nice people', on a more or less daily basis throughout your childhood you tend to believe that. My poor mother was saying that to me because she believed it to be true of her and she used that trick of projection onto me to help herself cope with her own inner trauma. I am pretty sure that this has shaped my attitudes towards tactful dishonesty more than anything else, but also taught me the importance of deep honesty.

What we say is more about our self than others – always. What we say about others to others is all based on our perceptions and judgments and not on any reality of that person being dissected. If you express judgments or criticisms you are showing yourself to the people you express them to, not the person you are talking about. But by collusion we forget that and instead collaborate in our discussions of the other in order to create a comfortable cocoon around our own judgments and insulate our self from our own nature and perceptual biases.

> *It is discouraging to think how many people are shocked by honesty –*
> *Noel Coward*

Tact suggests we are afraid to say what we really want to say, but are we afraid of our own judgements and/or of the other person's reaction/ response to them? Are we afraid of upsetting someone and would prefer to risk lying to them instead? Perhaps some people do not understand this as lying and instead think they are trying to be kind. So is tact really cowardice under a different hat?

Trying to be kind is an interesting concept; can you try to be something like kind? Surely you are either kind or not kind but trying to be kind suggests it is not coming naturally.

That is in itself a dishonesty that you might prefer but that the other person might not be worthy of.

Surely we all deserve someone to be honest with us, and you can be kind and honest at the same time.

How can I trust that you are really a kind person if you have to try to be kind instead of being naturally yourself, authentic and honest and raw as this might be? Perhaps we should say intending to be kind instead- but then is that the truth.

I can trust honesty and even respect not-nice-ness when it is honest, much more easily than I can accept and cope with tact and polite dishonesty. The latter makes my energy sensors go into overdrive and I will shut down. My amygdala just will do that, not from choice but from lack of trust. It depends too on the energy of the honesty.

Even the harshest criticism delivered skillfully can be infinitely more acceptable compared to a tactfully placed lie.

> ### *Honesty is the best policy, if I lose my honour, I lose myself*
> ### *- William Shakespeare*

Tact should be limited to honesty plus finding the right way to say something, or the best timing, a time when it will fit into the context and not jump out as an attack, a criticism, a condemnation.

At its most honest best this is the only positive thing that tact could ever be. This is to me an honest and mindful way of speaking.

Are we afraid of the truth about something?

We might not want to be the one to break the news, to challenge the recipient with some much-needed feedback or advice?

Are we afraid that our advice might be rejected with hostility or that our advice might be mistaken, which of course it may well be?

We all need to develop the humility to accept how our best advice and observations might be terribly wrong in some way and to accept that with good grace.

But they might be helpful and insightful and loving in their intention, well-meaning and respectful of the other's right to be human and thus not perfect.

Sometimes it is just what someone needs to hear and sometimes it just will not help someone; they are too old or too stuck or to afraid or too vulnerable to cope with this truth that we wish to impose on them for our own edification.

> *Honesty is the cruelest game of all, because not only can you hurt someone, you can hurt them to the bone, and you can feel self-righteous about it at the same time –*
>
> *Dave Van Ronk.*

Do you love or respect someone enough to be honest to them about themselves without unkindness?

Do you love and respect yourself to be honest with yourself and accept the love and honesty from another who would offer it to you?

Could you welcome their respect or chase it away with your defensiveness and anger and hostility?

Can the other cope with your honesty; do they have the support mechanisms in place or the internal systems to manage critical feedback?

It is how that honesty is given, the delivery, timing, motivation of the giver then matched with the maturity and stability of the receiver and the negotiated state of the mutual relationship that are the keys to a truly kind and mindful honesty.

Sometimes my sons say I am biased when I give them praise and I remind them how bluntly honest I can be so why would I change that for the positive feedback.

They know they can trust my joy at their successes in life because they know I am not tactfully polite, and I mean what I say.

Is this true tact in fact, what it was originally meant to be and just greatly misunderstood and misused? These I can cope with but how many people can actually be aware of these fine and subtle distinctions, this level of skillfulness. Well yes, we can all achieve this but only by dissecting honesty and tact in the first place and closely examining our personal integrity deeply.

Having grown up with a fiercely critical and judgmental mother and father, I learned from an early age to cope with verbal onslaughts. Being told that no one likes me but they are nice to me because they are nice people left me deeply distrustful of people for decades, all people, unless I found them to be brutally honest with me at other times.

Is my sensitivity to dishonesty rooted in my early damaged self and is it another blessing in disguise or have I got it wrong and am I too rigid in my need for clarity and honesty? Alternatively has that damage enabled me to highlight the fundamental dishonesty in most social interactions?

Another form of dishonesty I find challenging is based on the psychological concepts of cognitive dissonance combined with attribution bias.

This is when people clearly shift their story to fit the view that suits their self-narrative best of all, absolving themselves of responsibility, of being a victim of circumstances without the freedom to make moral choices and stances.

We all do this at some level or another.

Do you need to deny this as you read? See if you can hold it for a moment though.

I am aware that I have been guilty of this behaviour too and we all have. Who knows what the future holds and in this moment I am re-thinking these issues through on the pages as I write them?

The above combinations will attribute circumstances to their own 'bad' behaviour, as in 'it was out of my hands' but will blame someone else for not taking responsibility and making unskillful choices.

I have been in this kind of absolute conflict and it did cause an end to the relationships involved, the bias was all pitted against my narrative, so I preferred to just walk away with my own truth and let them get on with theirs. We shall never agree and agreeing to differ would not work long term. Sometimes this is the casualty of this very tricky issue and it creates so much unhappiness and yet is not explored in the great depth it needs as we grow up. The result is that many people are left with vague and defensive positions that are not explored deeply and are whatever they can live with. This is the basis for so many relationship breakdowns on familial and international levels.

If we seek to be honest, truly honest to our best ability, we can start with a very clear set of personal values or ethics. Mine are deeply rooted in my spiritual beliefs and experiences as well as what life has shown me. They have evolved over time and thus I am a very different person to 'she who I once was'; yet she is my root, at my core. I have given them a great deal of consideration over time and have walked away from many situations and relationships in order not to compromise them further.

We can seem to stand resolute but be battered by the whimsy of life and other people, and this is where the attribution bias slips in. 'It is not my weakness, but they made it impossible for me'. How much is this the truth? Is it not easier to say this than to say I was too afraid / angry / weak to make what would have been a more honest or fairer or respectful choice?

My mother lied all the time, without noticing it, and then completely denied it if challenged, with tones of incredulity that were astonishing to behold.

She was horrified by her own deep inner nature, her demons and the darkness that lay within her and her lies merely served to defend her flimsy sense of integrity. Can we blame her for that, and yet her lies did untold damage to others, caused suffering and abuse on quite extensive grounds?

I grew up with this role model and learned the art of lying for my own survival, the first line of defense against parents whose main aim in life seemed always to want to destroy me. But it always felt wrong inside, defensive, distancing me from those around me. Later my lies were to help me feel more interesting as a person, to seem to be able to cope with more that I could manage in reality, to cover-up my own failings. In other words, to protect an ego that had taken so much of a battering in its formation that it just struggled to survive.

How can we blame those for whom honesty is just too painful to cope with? How do we cope with those who need to keep a truth that we know is not consistent with what they say others should do, 'I lie because I have no choice, but you are a bad person to lie at all'!

This seems to me to be the worst kind of dishonesty, the double dishonesty of hypocrisy and deceit. And yet again can we judge those who resort to these tactics, have we ourselves done this ever?

In conclusion I think that real honesty is almost impossible.

Being as honest as possible means being open to your own faults, to accept other perspectives on your most cherished narratives about yourself and adopting a set of values which you know you can honestly stick with and not compromise on when the going gets tough.

And not fall into the many psychological dishonesty traps; to develop a non-judgmental and compassionate approach to life and to lose as much of your own ego as possible. This is one of the deepest Buddhist mindfulness teachings with personal and practical implications.

Travelling the Alphabet Emotionally

This issue lies at the core of my Buddhist heart.

Addendum – as an after-thought, if you need to be honest with or for yourself, but it means hurting someone else no matter what you do, do you have the courage to be true to yourself without looking back or do you quiver with fear about the guilt of hurting others and thereby hurt them and yourself even more. Sometimes honesty takes guts and risk – taking beyond what others might think of as acceptable. I think this self-honesty in your life is the most important thing anyone can do. And sometimes hurting others is the best thing you can do for them. That has been my experience, challenging but positive and educational. The honest alternative can only be Noble Silence.

Humility and humiliation

I shall be up front and open about this one as it is the only way to handle it – head on - otherwise I am giving in to my humiliation - and letting it win.

Humiliation is most often associated with shame, a devastating feeling about one's self.

It is mostly a combined lack of self worth and feelings of inadequacy, not being good enough and being unable to find anything good about yourself. I do regularly write positive things about the negative sides of life and how they help us to grow and I have experienced this effect personally – I always write from both theory and experience, with the emphasis on the latter so that what I write is as authentic as possible.

So I shall tell you about my own shame, its sources and manifestations, and how that is helping me to neutralise my self-denigration feelings. When people meet me for the first time, they usually really like me (or some really don't of course, I see myself a little like Marmite, love it or hate it).

BUT

I also have ADHD and the remnants of PTSD, and even at age 63 when I am writing this piece, I am not always able to manage the symptoms or behaviours they bring with them.

I have this deep anxiety, based on a combination of the two that however well people think of me, I will mess it up. In fact I prefer it when people don't think too highly of me; I can cope with liking a little bit but not too much.

The trouble is that people have expectations based on those first impressions.

Again I have written about expectations elsewhere, but to me they are a huge burden. I often unintentionally sabotage potential friendships because the weight of the expectations is just too great for me to cope with.

I find it utterly humiliating that I am not able to just cope and deal with things like other 'neuro-typicals' do. The shame kicks in when I try to join in, offer up my skills and services, and then I just mess something up as a result of my ADHD or my PTSD.

For example - not being able to 'not say things' or be too blunt. If there is an elephant in the room, I will point it out loudly even though everyone else wants to skirt around it more tactfully. They don't like me for that and are often cross or judgmental of me as a result.

For me the irritation is with people trying to say difficult things nicely, it just doesn't work.

I am not sure that is always a bad thing but because I am in the minority, that makes me wrong and everyone else right. My ADHD makes me utterly literal and that is how I both think and feel; what you see is what you get. I am hopeless at tact and being polite. If you want blunt open honesty, I am your friend, and I am a very good friend too. When push comes to shove, I am really there for people and surprisingly can get that pretty right, from a 'been there, done that, got the t-shirt, and written the books about it' perspective. I can work out what needs doing for others pretty well. But ask me to be tactful and I am not your woman at all. Those who love me actually love that about me the most. But those who do not like this approach to life, who do not understand it, they find me impossible. Sometimes my blurtiness (which is what I call it) gets me into trouble. I just don't see what is wrong with saying things that are true and without judgment, just how it is.

I forget that people react to their own inner judgements.

But sometimes I apparently mess up and say the wrong thing to the wrong people, which sets off a chain reaction that puts me in a bad light in the judgments of those others. It happens so often that I have to assume it is me who is in the wrong although I could contest that somewhat too! But it is humiliating to be in that position all the time, and de-moralising because no matter how hard I try not to be like that I just am and makes me feel hopeless.

How many times can a woman want the ground to open up and swallow them whole before that becomes a default position?

I can often sense what I got wrong soon after it comes out of my mouth and I get the horrendous creeping sense of dread for what will come next. But not beforehand! People with ADHD have real difficulty seeing consequences and this is true for me too. If it turns out that I have upset someone I am also devastatingly ashamed of my lack of management skills of my ADHD-ness and I really punish me. Then people start saying unkind things about me and/or get angry with me and that triggers my PTSD and I start to freeze up again, lock down, defenses on full alert. I start to hate myself for being how I am.

I never mean anything bad but somehow it is made to look as if I do it all willfully and on purpose. I am given malicious intent where there is none, but that really piles on the self hatred.

When I get into this cycle it puts me back into insomnia, self hatred, and the suicidal ideation/ self destruct thought patterns which have dominated my life.

But most of all I feel such humiliation and shame about my disability/ differences because of how people react to their expression.

Even though there are other aspects of ADHD that I love living with and which I think should be far more celebrated than they are globally, I am still crushed by its presence on a regular basis.

The shame is because these characteristics are intrinsically how my brain works and although I can get a handle on them for some of the time, like with all the more ADHD behaviours, if I am upset or anxious about something then it is far more likely that it will be out the door (my mouth), leaving me to writhe in shame and even more anxiety than before, because the thing I was worried about will almost certainly be the thing I am blurty about too.

And it may not matter but perhaps it will.

Over time I had become somewhat inured about some of my failings, and could just about cope with them, until my PTSD breakdown. This stripped me of all defenses and left me a total hollowed out wreck, broken open as completely as anyone can imagine, for about six years.

As I gradually ventured out into the world again though, and once I was free of the vice grip of full-blown PTSD, I hadn't reckoned with triggering. If people get angry with me about something that falls into this category, it triggers the deluge of self hatred and self abnegation, specifically the right to be alive as I am. That is easing over time, slowly.

It is more to do with the humiliating shame of other people's anger and judgments of me based on those tendencies. So if I then explain I have ADHD and can't help some of these issues then they are sympathetic and that is worse, I feel patronised and even more ashamed of being different. The bottom line is 'why did I have to have this brain'. It just doesn't register the normal kind of things that are useful in life which other people take for granted so much they don't even realise how good they are at it. But I can see how well they do this social acceptability stuff and can only gawp in awe and amazement.

Do I hate having ADHD?

No not really.

There are loads of upsides and there really tends to only ever be one of someone if they have ADHD- our own individual expressions of the alternative wiring makes for interesting combinations and variations on human self expression. I like that about me, it compensates for some of the more difficult stuff to live with.

But the shame of not being able to do basic fundamental social rule stuff really sucks. It makes you feel so stupid when everyone can see you are pretty intelligent, and that kind of makes it feel worse because you fail their expectations and then when they see how you are, they just pat you on the head (poor you – bit of a dead loss aren't you) at best or reject you at worst.

Can you respect someone for their cognitive disability?
Is it possible to be valued for exactly the bits you get wrong?

I think so, but it takes a little bit of joined up alternative thinking. I do need looking after, I am often very distracted and scattered, get myself into messes and such like, but overall, I can manage my own life pretty well.

My brilliant and deeply insightful husband is able mostly to help me without it ever feeling humiliating to be looked after and feeling infantilised, but is it in there too, just by my needing, and having to acknowledge that I need this help with everything.

We are all here to learn and to teach others. He says that I am here to enable him to give service to others. I wish it wasn't me but then is that my pride getting the in way. I should move from humiliation to humility, 'yes I am great at this but no I am useless in that, so please help me!'

Perhaps I am also here to enable others to hone their sensitivity skills, but mostly they don't see it that way, they just see me as a problem, and that is how they treat me.

Very humiliating.

In Native American spiritual teachings there is a character called Heyokah, the teacher of wisdom through opposites. Otherwise known as a trickster, the intention is that they are a person who throws a spanner in the works, with humour and by doing the opposite of what people want, or expect. At this point I am thrusting my hand up – 'I can do this, I can do this really well!!!

The job is in confronting them with their own limitations and narrow, normal thinking pathways.

The aim is always to do the opposite of what people think they want you to do but to do it with good humour and laughter, so that it is comfortable, if that is possible.

I think people like me are the Heyokah of now. We turn it upside down and show you how things really are, how shallow everything is when only looked at from one perspective. So if I break 'confidentiality' or say things that I am not supposed to say, perhaps that is what I am doing, being Heyokah.

I can honestly say that I am horribly honest and not very good at saying something that is not 100 per cent truthful as I see it. Of course I can be mistaken in my perspectives but never malicious or unkind. I can be reactive and blunt but only in honesty and good intentions. This is a Heyokah kind of behaviour. Many other cognitive disabilities, like Autism can manifest in the same way – direct and literal.

My sense of humour is mischievous and tends towards challenging social norms by nature. Again this is not willful but just how my character seems to express itself.

I am earthy and sensual, I like natural body smells and wild living, but also very private, open and straightforward, yet still so humiliated and ashamed of who I am; a woman of opposites, many of them as a result of life experiences.

For some people, laughing about my gaffs is not allowed. Instead I am often made to feel extremely foolish – like 'I fell down that hole YET AGAIN' – so I get it in first with the shame – before anyone can get cross or angry with me, I am onto it, again a result of so much shame programming in early life.

Humiliation doesn't help though – it doesn't make me stop having this issue with blurtiness, it doesn't make me a better practitioner of those immaculate social skills that some people display, and which also through experience I have learned not to trust - ever.

You might be good at saying things the right way, but I find it patronising you can't just say it straight and I fundamentally distrust people who are too good at this so-called social skill, to me it is too open to abuse of honesty and trust. I always rely on the sense of connected energy and if that is not there, I am not fooled

My first and best loved teacher of all things spiritual and psychological is Thich Nhat Hanh followed very closely by Pema Chodron. I think they would both say finding a way to accept and love yourself is the more important skill than beating yourself up for just being something that you cannot seem to get a handle on even though you have been trying about as hard as anyone ever tried about anything to achieve that skill – for over six decades - but it just doesn't happen and no amount of anger from others, rejection or anything else will change that.

It could topple me over into self destruct in a way that I can't hold back on though.

I will of course keep on trying but I also need to relax and just be me. I have no malice or ill intent and if I do inadvertently say something I should not say, but is actually true – well let me do a Heyokah on it and turn it on its head - perhaps we should all stop being so ashamed and secretive about our issues in life.

Perhaps Heyokah is showing everyone else that they are the ones who are wrong to think that confidentiality and secrecy are good things, when in fact they seem to me to reinforce shame in others too.

What are we all so ashamed of - that we messed up in our lives or we got sick or we did something we didn't oughta do.

Welcome to the club of all humanity. We all do it.

We should all just stop being ashamed of when we mess up and allow Heyokah to do its magic.

I didn't choose this body; it chose me - at conception.

I would probably not choose to be Heyokah in this culture- it's a very challenging role to play, but that is what I am, and I have to accept it.

Perhaps that is why I have ADHD and got PTSD too, so I could be a complex case of Heyokah and do a good job of it, a comprehensive job even.

Then perhaps I can stop feeling so ashamed of my openness and honesty, even if it is, at worst, a little indiscreet at times.

I know humiliation and shame are huge issues for so many people, so I hope you can find a way to think of yourself that will allow you to heal that wound and come to accept yourself a little more deeply. It works for me increasingly although every so often I hit a shame trip and have to ride it out. But with the wonderful teachings I have studied for so many decades now, I can honestly say I think this is my way out. This explains why I am like I am and why I have to be like this – just as we all are like we are, exactly like that, for a reason. We do and will all change too of course, but some things are just wired in the brain. And brain plasticity can only go so far – it cannot create areas that were never there in the first place, I don't think so anyway. And if that did happen it would no longer be me as I am. If I am meant to be Heyokah then that is what I must accept I am and do so with humility, accepting that I can never be anything great because whatever I am will always get messed up with the blurtiness.

Humility is the gold at the end of the rainbow in this one.

Shame and humiliation are both from ego / fear, and this little ego thing is not always our best friend, in fact mostly not our friend at all although it wants to appear so. Once we can move to acceptance of all we are, for better or for worse, then we can stop being so afraid of our Heyokah selves or those who express it around us and instead embrace them for the joy and wisdom they bring.

Find your Heyokah and find a way to enjoy it!   We can all be working on it together!

Intuition.

Intuition is the highest form of intelligence. I am often quoted on that and challenged too.

Trusting your Intuition was the title of my second book, the quotation came from there.

Did I follow my own advice? Yes, at least that is, and always was, my intention. Back then, before then, or even now, I confess I try my best to live as intuitively as I can. Sometimes I fail too!

As I get older and the evidence that intuition is more important than common sense or logic becomes clearer to me, I relax into that mind-set more easily. It has taken me years to fully trust my own advice, even though I once fervently believed it to be _the truth_.

The key word in that sentence is trust – a process of letting go of control, knowing, of being in charge, of being self-assured and certain about your route through life.

It is pretty much a given that your intentions and experienced outcomes do not always match – if they do then lucky for you, you were just intending what was already there, but for most of us that is not the case. Most of us find that life has very different ideas to our idyllic imaginary one and that can throw us thoroughly off balance and cause enormous distress if we do not see clearly the benefits of that experience.

We have our intuitive mind that wishes us to be happy and creative and wise, but also to learn what that means.

I emphasize here that wisdom is not information-based knowledge but insight; perception into how the world works, how to be happy, contented, fulfilled, with little or no reference to the material or concrete dimensions of experience.

To trust, that we will be ok, without those material and concrete certainties, takes a leap of faith that most cannot even attempt, and many prefer instead to seek for exactly that material concrete certainty with all its falsehoods.

Someone recently asked how I defined intuition. My response was that in many ways it is like Zen, like enlightenment, like love. You can't really describe it and if you think you can then you probably don't really understand it fully.

But you can gain an idea of what it is by what it is not, and explore the experiences you have had that might translate as intuitive.

How did they develop and how did you manage them; how did they feel? Feeling intuitive experiences is more important than thinking about them, since it is definitely not a cognitive experience nor a cognitive process, yet writing about it or reading, this is a very cognitive process.

So the nearest definition I can develop is this

'Knowing something without knowing why you know it or how you know it and often going against common sense or logical reasoning. Reading the energy of a situation or set of circumstances by sensing it rather than thinking about them.'

Examples in my own life are many and varied, but one thing they have in common, when I ignore that sense of knowing or that inner voice, which sometimes it literally is, I am always shown why that is wrong. Yet when I go against all logic and common sense and follow that inner voice, my life falls into all sorts of previously unimagined opportunities and adventures which come good.

One that still stands out to me was when it 'felt the right time' to step away from secure employment as a teacher/ lecturer; to let go and see where my individual qualities would take me.

I'd had several hearty nudges, verging on a good kick up the backside if I am honest, but this was when I was still tentatively learning how to use this approach to life consciously.

I was also a single mum with responsibility for two young sons to take into consideration, plus a huge mortgage.

Earlier in my life I had not considered myself particularly intuitive, but it had become apparent that I was being pushed and shoved to 'wake-up' to myself at a deeper level. These wake-up calls can be traumatic and unsettling; some of them were for me, that is definite.

In the intervening decades I have certainly travelled a long way. When I first wrote my book 'Trusting your Intuition' I was still in the first flush of recognising this wonderful gift and approach to life, and full of what I thought I knew. With the hindsight of experience and the aging process I am now far more experienced at living intuitively and using this approach constructively in my life and that of my family too. I also understand how little I 'know'!

There are a few crucial elements in living intuitively.

The first is to recognise what the voices of ego, anxiety, social convention, common sense etc. sound like and how that is so different to and yet will try and masquerade as, intuition.

I have upset a few people by not doing what they thought was sensible or the 'right' thing to do.

When I gave up my safe teaching job with pension, to go self-employed as writer and meditation teacher, an old school friend was very angry, almost contemptuous of me for not consulting her before making my decision.

But I knew she would dissuade me so I knew there was no point in asking her. I pushed myself to the limit financially and was at risk of losing my home and all sorts of things. But I didn't!

I was very, very scared too, so I did not need her 'support' phoning me weekly to help me worry about how it would work out. I had to ask her to stop doing that as she was making me feel very bad indeed. I was going through one of those complete life changes when everything dives in every direction but it all turns out to be a huge wake-up call, which meant I was changing, the dynamics between us were changing; I no longer did what she said I should do. I did once ask her for practical help but she quite told me off for that. The friendship did not survive sadly but if it had it would have become something very different, I was no longer going to do what she told me to do; I was growing and the friendship didn't adapt.

Is this intuition or just personal growth? Well it is both since intuition more often or not leads to personal growth.

Intuition is often left field, and nothing that would fit into the aforementioned lists. There is nothing logical about it. That is what is so wonderful and creative and adventurous about living intuitively. It is risky perhaps, if risking the odd failure is deemed too risky to countenance; it can lead to losses and being humbled. All this is good as it teaches you not to fear those possibilities because you do survive them, and this makes you braver and more resilient in the longer term.

Too many people never reach their best or their potential because there is too much fear in their life; too many reasons why they can't do this, or that. Failing is the greater part of success, but anxiety about that is widespread and very emotionally disabling.

There are various tools we can use which can help us access our intuitive knowing. I still very occasionally refer to tarot when I am feeling a little fuzzy and confused. T clarifies my thinking.

Nowadays I am just trying to settle my thoughts in the present moment though, not trying to divine anything about the future.

That is utterly dependent upon this present moment and how I manage my response to this present moment.

The future develops out of each present moment, so being fully and mindfully awake in the present moment is a wonderful way of knowing how it is probably going to evolve.

However the part you cannot know ever is
what else will happen around you.

We are never in isolation, we are all very much a part of everything else and totally dependent upon everything else. We cannot exist if everything else is not in place to support our existence but we can never be in control of that. We are certainly threatening our own existences by continuing to ignore global warming and pollution and ecosystem damage and climate change.

That I have known and sensed despairingly for decades, but so many people do not want to listen to that message and until we are all on board with it, I can only do my part in not contributing to it further.

But if I can clear my mind of fuzziness or work out what is causing the fuzziness, I can certainly clear a way through to the future being how I would prefer it to be. I can be clear about my motivations and wishes and also how they will make a contribution for others.

That is the closest we can ever get but that can be pretty powerful.

For instance I want to be happy as much as possible, like most people. If I make my happiness dependent on something external then I may be doomed to losing it too.

But if I make my happiness dependent on this moment and the richness of life in this moment, my breath, my consciousness, the sky, the wind, the sun, the air I breathe, then I am not likely to lose too much of my happiness in the whimsy of daily life.

Of course I am also happy because of the people I love so much but they do not make me happy, they help me to express it though, and that is a huge gift.

I would use Tarot to clarify what is in my mind right now and what that is co-creating for the next moment, to work out what is mulling around in the murkiness of unconscious mind or what is even in conscious mind that I am not recognising or wanting to admit. That final phrase is key, 'wanting to admit'. How much of what we think and feel do we prefer to not admit to because we would judge it and deem it beneath us or too scary or something around those two agendas in some shape or form.

 For instance at the present moment of writing this, my husband and I feel we are living in a Bardo, a limbo, a state of in between, while we wait to sell our house, and a life style that we have enjoyed for seventeen years, and move onto something that is more suitable to our physical needs as we enter the last two or three decades of living.

We don't know what we want to do next, where we want to live, what we want to live in, what we can still manage to do physically and for how long, and how well we will adjust to all that. So mindfully and intuitively I know that we only need to live in each moment as it is just now, to go from each activity and choice and be happy in that. And we do exactly that. And yet there are demands on us all the time from friends, family and each other to know what we will do next or what we want from it. The demand for certainty from others is exhausting and pointless.

Next evolves from this moment, always and irrevocably, but sometimes it is the number of 'nexts' that separate us from our potential futures that cause us discomfort. We want to know the longer-term future and we are uncomfortable not knowing that, and yet it is always ultimately unknowable, of course it is. And uncertainty brings anxiety or adventure, that is the element of choice we have.

If we take an attitude of adventure towards life, we no longer need to fix down certainties. Living intuitively is really about sensing the energy of a moment, of the person, of the circumstance and never needing to fix down the certainties of life but instead feeling our way through it, warts and all. So I did a tarot reading for a month by month breakdown of the coming year and then I did another one a few months later on, both about the house sale. They both suggested that we would know something concrete by the summer but not what it was we would know. (That came true.) That should be enough and largely for me it is entirely enough. The future is on its way but for now I have plenty to keep me occupied in the present moment and that unfolds each day.

Two other words which block intuitive approaches to life are hope, and dream. They both want things to be something other than the way they are. Some people think you must have dreams to move you forward, just as you must have hope that things will 'get better' or at least 'be ok'.

The problem with both of these is that they are rather non-accepting of 'how things are at this moment' being 'as good as it needs to be', and they both place responsibility for the future externally, thus they potentially disempower us on all fronts.

We want something different. We don't like 'how it is' right now!

That is how intuitive living is sometimes misconstrued, putting it under the heading of fortune telling and hocus pocus. This reduces intuition to a sub-valued commodity or approach to living, when as I have said before and others too probably, I believe intuition is the highest form of intelligence and it is not based on intellect. It is sensory, left of centre, right field, out of the box, random, creative, and full of potentials to create, full of risks to take, chance combinations, and creative randomness at its best.

To support that claim is not so hard either really.

Intelligence at its highest is linked with innovative thinking, scientific, creative or social advancements. Flashes of intuitive genius need to be supported by ongoing thought and process, to form a more mental framework, these 'flashes of genius' are the intuitive input into the process.

The fact that the rest is ordinary or even extraordinary brain process demonstrates how much the mind is just a very useful back up tool to intuitive inputs. So I might have a flash of intuitive insight into a possible future plan for us in our change of life process. I would need mind to follow that through but the original flash of inspiration comes from a place that is easily dismissed as wishful thinking or delusional.

The flashes of intuitive realisation are more than that though because they have power in them, potential in them, and they stimulate action, without which a dream remains its fictional self, just a dream. I have at least a couple of such flashes daily. Sometimes they inspire me to write a piece or to say something, occasionally they offer suggestions about our next step. I listen to them, make note of them, and then let them lie for a while, until I have been able to assess their potential and practicalities. I never dismiss them. In the past I have always jumped to their tune and rarely failed completely but have been challenged to my core many times, since that is also their purpose, to challenge us and test us and force us to change our internal cognitive paradigms.

I want to do that now still but I have also learned that to live like that takes resources that I may not have any more, such as energy and physical resilience which I have lost in huge amounts since my breakdown.

But I also know intuitively that if there is a certain direction to go in, then those considerations will be resolved one way or another, and I will be supported in that process by unseen energies.

I am not talking about predetermined options either here; I am not deterministic in thinking at all. That is also a blocking non-intuitive approach to life.

Instead I am saying hold all options in your open mind and allow them to fall or flourish as circumstances dictate. So currently I have about six options, all of which have pros and cons to them and between which I have chosen to keep an equally open mind. When the time is right the best option will put its best foot forward and fall into place. It may even be none of the above at all, but it will be clear and available, it will open itself to me as a gift, a flower opening to the early morning sunshine, a new possibility. Then I will intuitively know and accept that this is the best choice. It will 'feel right' even when I don't like the first impression of that option.

The best choices in life then are the ones that come intuitively, even if they do not lead to greatness, success, huge wealth or status. Our intuition is wiser than that and knows these are false dreams, false options, false outcomes that bring with them illusions that almost certainly eventually show their intrinsic worthlessness. The best choices bring insight, wisdom, mindfulness, compassion, peacefulness.

Our intuitive mind knows we have to understand many things in order to find true happiness. In order to reveal that, it sometimes has to show us what happiness is not, to bust the illusions and delusions we hold so dearly, to blow them wide open and destroy them at our feet so that we cannot reclaim them once again, unless we are completely blinded to intuitive wisdom. But if you live intuitively you can see the teaching in everything that happens, that we learn from the cause and effect (Karmic) laws of the universe and physics.

Having one's life busted open from time to time is a good way of intuiting that you need to be more open and accepting of life experiences.

You need to make more changes within yourself.

Perception is an important part of living intuitively because it necessitates an examination of the 'how' and 'what' of our perceptual template for living. If you omit an intuitive perceptual stance from life you will not see it or interpret events within its terms of reference and instead attribute them elsewhere. That doesn't mean that intuition is an illusion but rather it is a choice of ways to perceive as well as a way to live. My reasons for choosing it are many.

Firstly it has shown me many times that whilst there are those who would decry and diminish my approach to life, there is little if anything in their lives that I would rather have. Their alternative offers me nothing that I want in addition to what I have and have had as I stand in this moment. So their lives work for them but my life works for me. We all have off days, that is allowed but overall, I am content with this reality

I want to live freely. It is my conscious choice to live more freely, more mindfully awake and aware, and more intuitively. It is a choice that is open to anyone who also would like to live like this but it is not the only way to live.

I want to live openly and acceptingly. Once upon a time I might have felt quite strongly that this was the _best_ way to live because I could see no attraction in the lives of others. But I have now learned deeply that each of us is in a position to make our own life paradigm choices, whether consciously or unconsciously, and neither is right or wrong, just different. It is through my work teaching mindfulness that I realised how many people were as unhappy as I used to be before I embraced this approach to life but it is up to them to find that out for themselves and often the very reason they are coming for mindfulness classes was to begin reassessing that choice for them self.

Even that perspective does not convince me any further that I am right to live this way and others are mistaken not to, it just shows me that each choice has its outcomes.

So living intuitively is an expression of how we view life, of being awake and aware in the present moment, of living mindfully with compassion and openness.

It is liberating and challenging in equal measure. It asks you to let go of certainties and to take risks, to experiment and explore, to have courage and value the intrinsic worth of everything just as it is, to make choices and take responsibility for those choices but to also understand that we are victims of our biology and history to the extent that we cannot recognise and release them.

I have a lot of pain from a damaged spine but I have managed to establish a dialogue with my nervous system that allows me to bargain with it in terms of how much pain it needs to send me and why and how I can listen to it better so our communication has the desired outcomes for us both, me and my nervous system. At the moment I accept that pain is the messenger that reminds me to sit well, to support my back, to keep moving but be mindfully aware without tensing against the pain, never to see the pain as something to reject or be upset or angry about, but to value it as a friend who is helping me keep mobile for as long as possible, to minimise further damage and to be the best carer I can be to my own physical body. Thank you pain for working with me intuitively to keep my life as good as it can be.

Living intuitively had been a fantastic adventure that has taken me to places many will never know or even want to visit. The only limit on it has ever been fear and that has never served me particularly well. Fear has made life dark and hollow and I question the value of life lived in fear, so without intuitive living, well, who knows?

Jealousy and Envy - facing down the green-eyed monsters

Almost identical twins but there are a few slight differences.

Jealousy is far more complicated than envy, and also incorporates it more often than not, so I shall look at that one first. Jealousy is caused by a mixture of fear, anxiety, insecurity, abandonment issues, humiliation and general low self esteem. It can also include envy. It is a powerful weapon to use and manipulate against someone, and yet it often is, through accusation, flaunting, taunting and other generally unkind behaviours.

Envy is more straight-forward and is just more or less resentment against somebody else that has something you want.

Jealousy and envy are both potentially destructive of relationships, and whole lives even. None of this is necessary once we can unpick them.

My first experiences with jealousy are firmly rooted in my early childhood so this section is largely biographical, to put my understanding into context.

I recall being told by my mother that I was jealous of my sister, and then being sneered at for it. I was about four or five yrs old, and didn't know what that word meant but I knew, from the jeering way she spoke, that it was not good in her eyes and just one more reason why she should reject me utterly. So I denied I was jealous.

What I do remember feeling was confusion, and uncertainty, - that actually I loved my little sister deeply and didn't understand what this word meant, but clearly I was bad in some way.

But looking back I don't think I was jealous of my sister because I felt sorry for her and wanted to defend her from our mother's emotional abuse.

I felt responsibility, frustration, disappointment and many other emotions including anger with my sister, but never jealousy as far as I can recall.

As a very young child, I was myself filled with anxiety, fearful of abandonment, experienced regular public humiliation by my mother and had a vast sense of worthlessness. I saw that my sister had many of the same things developing in her, but I lacked the envy component of my sister in ways that meant I was jealous of her.

My sister and I are very different people as adults, hardly identifiable as sisters in approach to life, and not close at all anymore. But I think as children we were. I remember being kind to her often because I wanted to make sure she didn't go through what I went through. That is more compassion rather than jealousy, though like all older sisters I did find her annoying at times too. The older we got the less I wanted to be anything like my sister so jealousy was not the issue for me as far as I can tell- but perhaps it was suppressed.

What I realised many decades later was that my mother was insanely jealous of her two younger sisters and full of self pity and self hatred which are components of her narcissism. She had started projecting her feeling for herself onto me at a young age and this was just another one of those instances.

So when did I feel jealousy, or envy even - well not really, except once!
I shall come back to that later on.

Many years later, my sister accused me of being jealous of her and it struck me as so funny that I burst out laughing spontaneously. I wanted nothing that she had in her life, I didn't share the same values, the same politics, the same life paradigm, anything.

I didn't want anything about her life at all. But I think she was doing what mother had always done and that was to project her feelings onto me – i.e. she was jealous of me.

But why I don't know.

I have my suspicions but that is not for this book.

It intrigued me. It also started to liberate me because I realised that I had been told so many negative things about myself that had made me feel ashamed of myself and suddenly I realised most of them were just not true, they really weren't.

Amazing.

So when did I feel active jealousy, with all the trappings of anxiety and insecurity and lack of confidence? It was with my sons. I had been their main parent since they were small and their Dad and I went our own ways. He was not an engaged parent emotionally, he just didn't know how to be, like too many men who were brought up in the good old sexist ways of the 1950's and 60's. He was and still is, a well intentioned, kind man.

So my sons put a lot of effort into seeking their dad's approval and recognition, and I was taken for granted because I was just their solid rock foundation who would always be there for them.

They took me for granted out of confidence and thoughtlessness, not because they did not value me equally. They also had their dad as a male role model and thus a lack of engagement emotionally too. Plus I can be a very forceful personality and they had to keep their distance from me, I get that.

But I felt jealous of the effort he got and the lack of effort I got by contrast. And it felt dark, it felt bad, it felt like it could eat away at me if I let it, it made me snippy and defensive and worst of all, I didn't know how to manage it because I genuinely had not felt this nasty emotion before. I got defensive and snippy with my sons too.

I used my mindfulness skills to challenge it to show its face to me. I talked about it with my husband and life mirror, and together we brought it all out into the open light and looked at it and saw what was there.

And it was pure fear and a historical low confidence in their loyalty or love. Nothing to be ashamed of, nothing to reject or judge myself over.

Instead I was able to take myself in hand and heart and say not surprised you feel like that – understandable, but not helpful to you or them.

My sons were alerted also that I was briefly unhappy and were lovely and loving as ever and we are all through it now. They were also able to recognise something positive for themselves in this too.

But that was my brief yet full on meeting with jealousy and envy and it was not pleasant. I really feel for people who get eaten up by this one and we should be able to talk about it more openly because its basis is such a damaged and damaging space to inhabit for anyone.

Can we learn to embrace this duo in a more positive healing way than judging someone for feeling like this?

Can we feel compassion for them?

Can we see that it is a deep affliction born from many wounds and hurts, the thousand cuts that life can inflict on us all, be gentle with each other?

Can we all be more open and understanding about the power of these two emotions so that they can be soothed and healed more readily?

I like to think this is possible through education, through conversation about these issues, through openness about how we each may be afflicted in this way. I like to hope we can do and people reading this article will be a little kinder to each other afterwards, and to themselves.

I want to put in a small addendum here- aspiration – seeing what others have and wanting for yourself but not resenting it for them, is OK as long as you know what your motivation for that aspiration might be. If it is jealousy, then work to release that emotion, but if it is for self betterment in terms of your expression of self, then go for it.

Aspirations are needed to make the world a better place- as long as that is the motivation behind it.

Joy and Happiness

Who doesn't want to experience joy and happiness in their life?

Where can we find it though?

As a child growing up, I thought that both parents wanted to deprive me of as much joy and happiness as they could manage, because that was how it felt.

Of course they didn't intend that at all and probably didn't consider my happiness or joy in any way. It wasn't part of parenting ideology at the time.

But that sent me on a journey to understand what joy is and where we find it.

It is a journey that still hasn't ended but it has been great and I have learned some amazing stuff along the way. Well they seemed amazing to me as I learned them because they were complete and astonishing revelations, but to many people they were already known. That is the point – we all have to discover these life lessons for ourselves or at least have them introduced.

I discovered that there was a permanent store of Joy, deep inside me, and it was always just waiting to be let out of its prison, the bars of which were the delusions and illusions of life.

The point of it is that I was made to feel so utterly despicable and unlovable by my parents, I'm surprised I ever did find joy inside myself at all. But there it was, and out it popped at odd moments.

Looking back I realise now that those moments of joy were ones where I forget myself and was just in a state of pure being. I was on my bicycle with the wind in my hair racing along seeing how fast my child's legs to get me, or I was up a tree climbing to the highest branches that could possibly take my weight and gently swaying there in the breeze.

Or lying on the grass watching toadlets and froglets bravely make their way from the ponds down by the river Trent where I used to live as a child, out into the big scary world where they were going to get eaten in their hundreds.

Those moments of joy made their mark on me. They were the glimpses of something beyond the reality of my uncomfortable childhood. I now recognise them in the terminology of Zen as sartori and pure mindfulness or samadhi. I glowed with joy then, until I had to close it down to come home. Best not let that be seen and risk it being attacked.

These moments called me on into life, into living. They helped me to feel grateful to the trees I was frequently challenging to end my life by dropping me, for keeping me safe, always. I could forever return to their woody embrace and feel connected. I can still feel that connection too. Trees definitely helped me - with their slow, deep, woody ways - to find the joyful reality of life underneath all the debris.

Joy wants to be found. It is just waiting for us to uncover its secrets, to jump out and say 'boo' to us in unexpected moments, IF WE LET IT!

Finding joy is a process of letting go of that emotional debris which collects like leaves on a path in autumn. It is simply the collection of past memories, hurts and injustices, beliefs and thoughts that we continue to take hold of and accept as real. That is our mistake, and once you can understand this, joy is much easier to access.

This secret about joy, it is waiting to be found.

And enjoyed - this needs to be spread far and wide.

This should be the central message in schools everywhere – life is joy if you know how to let it out of the cupboard.

Life is not about striving to be better or bigger or richer or more famous – it is about finding joy and living with it.

Everything is interconnected and nothing is worth any less than anything else, the saying really applies.

'no mud no lotus'

Once you have joy everything else flows from there and life becomes whole and real and worth living for every joyful second of it. Once you recognise joy, even suffering gets put into context and makes more sense so it is less painful to live through.

I still get the echoes from the past invading my joy nowadays. Sometimes they even throw a blanket over me and it is a struggle to find the edges, so I can climb out from under it again. But I know that joy is there and I will always grow towards it, and away from that which wishes to hold me back. Joy is our bedrock, we just have to excavate down to it.

Kindness

Kind can be a bland word. It is slightly better than nice though. Kind is a doing word, and an adjective. So you can act kindly or be described as kind. In either role it is far more important than is recognised.

Kindness, the simple act of being kind, is so often overlooked in current times. Certainly our politics is not kind at all; in fact it has become increasingly unkind. Or maybe that is an illusion and it was never kind but we didn't know about it so much. But with the immediacy of information nowadays, even attempts to cover unkindness have been largely abandoned and instead dressed up in terms of 'no options' other than to act in this way or make that decision. Of course that is never true. There is always a choice and there are always options. And to each option there are always pros and cons. But kindness seems to have dropped off the radar completely in all areas of public, political, and social consideration.

Kindness, the act of being kind, is about not doing harm.

It incorporates qualities of ethical behaviour, compassion and empathy, gentleness, selflessness and a general sense of well-being directed at others once we have learned to direct kindness to ourselves first. It is seen as a virtue by many religions and cultures but it is left un-promoted nowadays by the media. When did you last see a politician or significant media presence of any sort, described as 'kind'?

Kindness is a behaviour that comes from an attitude and a state of inner being. The attitude is that of taking care of others before self, of being less ego-centric. This has been significantly underplayed as a positive attribute in the last four decades or so, as the cult of the self has taken over.

Since kindness necessarily requires that self comes second, it has dropped out of clear sight.

So to get this into perspective. First of all we all have an ego which is necessary for us to live with. However too many people have ego's which are out of control and utterly self-focused. When this happens it is called Narcissistic Personality Disorder and is noticeably present in many political leaders. I will talk about that in more depth later on in its own chapter. But for the purposes here I am only talking about normal levels of self.

We need to take care of ourselves and meet our own needs physically, emotionally and socially. Once we can do that, we have a more or less stable relationship with life, and achieving this goal is supposed to coincide with the transition from child to adult. However in most people the ego is damaged and left undeveloped at best and distorted out of shape at worst. We have lost the ability to be kind to self along with the understanding of what being kind means

Kindness is a quality we need to learn for our own sakes too, since we just become a problem for others and place demands on them that may not be met anyway if we do not learn to self care through self kindness.

Kindness is an essential life skill.

I need to look after me so I am not a burden on others. That then frees me up to care for others with the spare capacity, once I have taken care of my own needs. If I try and look after others without making sure I am good first then I risk using the care given as a buy, a basis for demands, an expectation for that pound of flesh back at a later stage, further down the line.

Travelling the Alphabet Emotionally

That is not kindness.

I knew someone and I have also done this myself in the more distant past, where they went out of their way to be the perfect friend. BUT in this case, they would not accept a response in kind and if one was given then it was returned again immediately, whereas to leave it would have been enough and allowed us both to enjoy giving to each other. Instead it turned into a competition. I stopped responding, I hadn't got the energy to keep it up and it became a chore instead of the joy it was meant to be. Kindness is giving without agenda and learning to receive too. The 'kindness to yourself' part. The minute it gets into competitive realms it is not kindness it is 'Buy' or another agenda- 'you have got to like me look what I do for you'.

If we are kind to ourselves then we do not need approval from others or make demands from them, and anything they do give us is just a gift, a joyful exchange, not a buy or anything else. If and when we do need a favour we can also ask without fear of reproach, then, or later on.

Kindness is being there for someone without your own agenda.

It may even be a stranger who you will never meet again. I once helped some people out when they were stuck in a difficult situation. I did it because I felt for them and was able to help, and I liked them. But they were not from this country so I had no expectations from that gesture.

Nearly thirty years on we are still great friends and help each other out all the time, but I still feel absolutely no sense of whose turn it is or any other agenda, we each do what we can when we can for the other out of friendship and kindness.

I have had friends who expected me to 'be there for them' when I didn't have the capacity and have since dropped me as 'I let them down'. Their perception of kindness was based on expectations and had its own agenda thus in my interpretation is not true kindness. You may disagree.

In many ways kindness is incorporated in altruism but it is simpler than altruism which has far deeper philosophical roots. Kindness is simply being gentle with people. It is, - well –it is being kind.

If we can do one kind act each day it will make such a difference to others around us, and that in turn makes us nicer people, happier, more confident and relaxed.

There was a wonderful film called Pay It Forward. If we always wait for someone to do something kind for us first then we may wait a long time. If we start and they don't respond perhaps they are not able to. That doesn't matter. Somewhere down the line they may be kind to someone else who cannot return it to them either. The point is that somewhere that kindness was passed on.

The opposite of kind is cruelty at its extreme or just plain thoughtlessness in its lesser incarnations. Sadly I can think of far more evidence of cruelty in politics nowadays in UK and USA and elsewhere than I can think of basic kindness.

I grew up in a family where kindness was used as a word but not put into action very much at all.

There is a saying being cruel to be kind and I used to subscribe to that thinking. But now I doubt it has any valid efficacy.

Travelling the Alphabet Emotionally

Sometimes we have to make a stand about demands and expectations made of us, or say no, but we can still do it kindly, or tactfully as possible, without being unkind about it. Kindness can be used to be unkind, i.e. rejecting, in this situation, and thus is not worth the risk. Honesty, done well, can be challenging but is never unkind.

Sometimes we can see that someone needs our help. They have fallen in the street or something like that, or are stuck without enough money to get home or without food and shelter even. How we respond to these people is also a measure of how kind we are individually and as a society too. Although rushing to help is not always the best proposition in all of these scenarios, the fact homeless and those reduced to poverty still exist in well off countries means we do not live in a kind culture any more.

My experience is of wanting to be kind and feeling uncomfortable if I am put in situations where I cannot be obviously kind. I want to express my feelings of love for all living beings, but sometimes my fear, or defensiveness, takes over and I am unable to be endlessly kind. I hope that others will be kind enough towards me to understand that I am doing my best.

Kindness is so simple but seems to be so out of fashion nowadays and I think we have lost something very important. When you grow up with deep unkindness you can go either of two ways.

You can learn to behave like that too, and get caught in its insidious traps one way or another, or you can choose not to repeat that, knowing how it feels to be on the receiving end, and make sure you do not perpetuate unkindness. I also know that I have fallen into the former trap more times than I care to recall and I regret that deeply but I would not repeat that so I have learned the lesson. That is all we can ask of ourselves.

Letting Go

Letting go is a term often bandied about without people actually understanding how much of a challenge this process can be. 'Let it go' they say 'just let it go'.

What they really mean is 'stop talking about it or bothering me with it'. Oh if it were that easy for us all.

Most of our lives are spent accumulating things, ideas, beliefs, knowledge etc, when in reality we should be letting most of this go. Instead we should accumulate wisdom.

We are all born into a culture and family value system which moulds our understanding of the world and how we relate to it. The world is literally how we see it, thus there is no single reality world as such. These learned interpretations of experience are often a huge problem for us all.

For me, letting go came in stages.

Firstly to recognise that I had to let go of stuff, and then later, what that involved me actually doing.

I had to re-evaluate the family values, which were based in wealth, property size and value, status of career and external appearance. My parents had these values so fixed in their own minds.

So at a very early age, when I spontaneously began to challenge their core values, it caused a lot of deep anger and a breaking down of relationships.

By the time I was an adolescent and I was still very unskilled in ways of confronting these issues, things resulted in even more damaged relationships.

In my heart, my underlying intention was to change the values so we could all have better relationships, but at 15 – 18yrs I was unable to articulate this well.

But I was unable to relinquish what I felt was an essential and eternal truth, and that my parent's values were deeply mistaken. There were many other complications which I've mentioned elsewhere, involving letting go of ever more layers of assumptions, expectations, beliefs and perceptions. With each one, a newly evolved version of 'me' emerged.

I really thought I was reaching the end. That was yet another assumption I would have to let go of.

The crux came when I hit my mid fifties and what was left of my birth / extended family fell apart completely.

My father had finally cut me off at 19 yrs old and refused to see me again until just before he died. It was not a successful meeting, which triggered Post-Traumatic Stress Disorder that was later diagnosed having originated around 3- 4 yrs old. This persisted for 6 years and healing involved so many more layers of letting go in fine detail, its own gift. I had to let go of my cherished wish for a healing reconciliation before he died.

My mother also cut me in and out of her will so many times that I felt like a yo-yo but eventually a groomer came and took most of her final wealth anyway, so that was my relationship with family wealth. My siblings and I were left with the remainders after everyone else got their 'gifts' from her. Another form of letting go!

Just as I had struggled with my birth family values, I also had to let go of ideas of religious doctrine being something that one should blindly follow. They just did not match my experience.

I embarked on a journey that led me through politics, philosophy and into new age spiritual pathways before I realised that the only way to make life understandable was to go within.

Thus began a new stage in that journey of letting go.

I had to start letting go of much darker things here: my anger, my fear, desolation, a sense of utter worthlessness and being someone that no one could ever love, deep PTSD terror rooted in that early childhood experience, and a darkness that cloaked me.

Finally I released any victimhood, a delicious mixture of frustration at being 'right' and thus so misunderstood, anger at those involved for not adopting my set of values instead and sadness at the destructive path this had taken, including my own early unskilfullness at navigating it that assisted in creating these outcomes, my passion and desperation at times making me equally intransigent, clearly a family characteristic.

I have since replaced those qualities with gratitude for being where I am in my life now and understanding that the whole journey was necessary to bring me to this point.

The significant and near final letting go of those family values and agendas took place using the touching the earth for the ancestors at retreats, first with a Dharma Charya at New Barn and then shortly afterwards the same exercise with senior monastic Sister Annabel. These two are both senior teachers within the Plum Village tradition. It was the right time for me too, I was desperate to let it all go and be free from it all. The constant PTSD feelings just vanished. I had let them go too, as I thought.

But that experience of letting go was not just the PTSD easing back. Something else took over.

Moments of sartori became increasingly extended until they became almost constant and along with the PTSD and the final release of family issues went any 'sense of self' developed since I'd frozen myself at about 3-4 yrs old, along with all temporal experiences beyond the moment and all attachments. Confusion reigned for approximately 10 months. I lost emotional connections with my husband, children and close friends, with the contents of my life and with any sense of purpose.

I had realised aimlessness in the Buddhist sense, and a deep connection with the source, whatever you want to call it, god, nirvana, and delusion even! I am not attached to terminology.

But by now this was happening *to* me and there was nothing I could do to stop it. Things were shifting so often and the only option was to wait until this too passed although it was not always pleasant or comfortable. It left my husband and I confused, and me scared at times. We were only able to cope because our long-committed relationship was based on studying the Dharma.

It came with a sense of relentless bliss and I felt happy indeed but also totally confused. I had just wanted to let go of PTSD. The rest of it was more than I understood and no one seemed to be able to help me to cope or understand what on earth one does when this happens.

It is actually quite terrifying and yet one is in a state of bliss, impossible to explain this contradiction. Fortunately like all things, this too passed and I now feel grounded and able to function 'normally'.

My lovely husband managed to hold onto the journey too and things slowly settled down. Knowing that this thing can happen does not prepare one for its eventuality in such a dramatic way but there it is, there is now a quietude about everything, it all 'just is', 'this is it'. But what a choice – to let go of perpetual bliss or to let go of those I love. In the end love won through. This human life is a previous gift and should not be avoided. There is nothing to do except just be in this moment where the lights are fully on and all is bright and clear. There are new challenges, I am fully aware of that, but at the moment there is also no sense of needing to strive for anything ever again. It is very peaceful indeed. My only ambition is to share this journey, my story, and make it open to as many who want to know.

Love

That much needed key essential in all our lives that is about the most misunderstood emotion possible. Yet we are all sure we know what we are talking about and we assume we all mean the same thing, but in various experiences throughout my life I now realise that it is a vastly different concept for each of us, although there are also commonalities.

I learned all about love in ways that are the opposite of what is usually expected. I learned about the lack of it from my childhood. From that I learned what love truly meant. Sometime this is the best way around to fully appreciate such a gift.

When I was at school, apart from mostly finding it mind-bogglingly boring and limiting, I had the occasional lesson that inspired me and which I've never forgotten. One was a particularly lazy English teacher who did not prepare her lessons but just came into classes and talked to us or got us to read out loud and discuss, both of which I actually could engage with. (I said lazy, not bad).

The lesson I never forgot is the most basic philosophical question; if I look at this pen and you look at this pen and we both call it a pen, how can we know we all see the same thing.

Of course we can't and won't ever be able to. Even if we use the same words to describe our experience, we can never be sure since we may also be using and understanding the same words differently too.

It was my first introduction to the idea that truth is utterly subjective, world view is subjective and that my parents view of me might also be subjective; that what they called love was in fact not love at all, not as I understood it at least, and certainly not as I understood it from all the books I read, compared to the reality of living with their regime.

I realised quite early on that they did not in fact love me at all but they used that word to justify their treatment of me to themselves.

It has given me a lot to reflect upon concerning the issue of understanding love.

I grew up feeling that the worst sin I committed was to continue to live, a message reinforced so regularly that I could not mistake it, that I was an anathema to my parents and my existence only continued because they loved me in some way in spite of how abhorrent I actually was to them. This was what I grew up understanding as love, being told was love.

Far too many people experience similar and that needs to be challenged. That teacher, when I was around twelve years old, probably more or less saved my life; she gave me a reason to stop believing them and to fight back for myself, which is what much of this whole writing project is about, my journey from darkness towards the light, and how others can choose this path for themselves and heal their own lives.

So I am only sharing with you my own experience of what love is and what love is not. If you can relate to it, that's great, if not then I am interested to hear about it, to expand my understanding further.

I believe my parents possibly did love me when I arrived in human form on planet earth in 1955, but that love was so full of expectations and demands and intentions and needs that I was doomed from the start. Thus I would also challenge that emotion not as being love but as being all the things people call love, and which, sadly, destroys love.

I have deep compassion for both my parents since they did not understand love at all and their neediness destroyed our family and each other. They both did find love in other relationships, but not until they had inflicted great hurt and unkindness on each other and their children in varying degrees.

So is love about compatibility?

Perhaps! Was I just incompatible with my parents even though I was genetically so close to them? I believe there is more to it than that.

We meet someone and fall in love with them, we have compatible needs to be met and provided. If that balance is met there is some harmony but only if no-one shifts too much as an individual in terms of their emotional and spiritual growth. In other words the love is based on a foundation of rigid stasis which can crack at any time. It is therefore superficially stable but not thoroughly and deeply secure and grounded.

Is that love? Who can say, but I would argue it is more about need than love, and the needs being met induce the oxytocin effects that we mistakenly call love, plus a sense of relief and sanctuary and acceptance that are probably component parts of what I might call real love. But this rigidity often means that complete intimacy of heart and mind cannot be achieved because there are conditions on that balance, to keep it in place, and an implicit understanding of 'I won't go there if you don't either'.

It is often easier to explain and discuss what love is not, rather than what love is, which I shall come onto later.

So having realised I was not loved by my family, I still had that gnawingly empty ache to be loved inside, all the time. It was unknown by me at that time because I knew nothing else, but I recognise it now. Too many people know this also. Some do not recognise it inside themselves and sometimes it is only when it's gone that you can look back and say – 'that used to feel really bad'.

A friend once said to me, many decades ago now, that each soul has a mate somewhere in the world and they are always searching to find each other, neither can rest until they do meet, and sometimes it takes many lifetimes.

I found my soulmate in this lifetime.

I think I knew him before because he felt so familiar to me when we met and there was no falling in love heady romantic mixture, just a quiet sense of knowing and belonging that neither of us has questioned since, and completely different to anything or anyone else I have ever grown close to in whatever way.

The journey to get here took many turns but included some of the following:

Thinking that my desperation meeting someone else's desperation meant we were destined to be together- not a good recipe for a relationship and not love.

Thinking that someone who found me attractive, either sexually or socially; or in some personal way had expectations of me, would be a good friend / partner etc. – not a relationship on any level that would feed me but just based on their need to glean whatever they could from me until I ran out or said no more to them.

Thinking that someone who found me amazing would not let me down – falling off pedestals is a long drop and is also a form of imprisonment, not for my benefit or gain at all. Not love.

Thinking that someone who wanted me as a status in some way because of my looks or being interesting company or something that they could gain from me – but rarely had that much to give in return when the chips were down or when I again failed to deliver.

Thinking that being needed would make someone appreciate me and return the favour, never worked since all I found was that they took until I ran out and then they dropped, judged, or left, or in some cases ridiculed. When people are attracted to you, befriend you, and then simply want to compete with you to show that they are somehow better than you, thus you are in almost constant conflict and combative mode.

This is exhausting and means you are rarely able to give or receive with any true generosity. They will also use your low moments to massage their own superiority.

People who find my slightly wacky ways as being of passable value as a class clown, the royal courtly fool, not to be valued but just occasionally be amused by.

There are some variations along these themes of so-called friendship or love, and I am sure many more stories to tell. Of course I do remember that I was also very needy and hollow inside, so by the laws of energy attraction this is what I attracted towards my 'self' until I learned to change that inner energy. I am not judging anyone here, just stating lessons learned along the way

I learned that loving your 'self' means investing in yourself, your time and effort to heal and change, to turn negative energy into loving compassionate energy. I have taken a long journey into the discovery of what love is and I have found the following:

It takes effort and humility, openness and willingness to change and adapt to each other.

It takes acceptance of the whole person, recognition that we are each a process rather than anything fixed, that we all evolve even if we don't recognise it or try not to, and that this is the most crucial process in living a meaningful life together, the joy of the mutual development and the discovery of who we might each become.

For some this seems threatening (they see it as 'if you change, I can't control you any more, get what I want from you any more, where do I stand with you now').

But real changes occur as an adventure to find out 'who' the other will be when the transformation unfolds, and that person will be a whole new adventure to learn about and live with.

It is what keeps a relationship new and fresh every day. It stops us becoming complacent and routine. It keeps that relationship or friendship alive and vibrant no matter how long you have been together.

It takes courage to stay strong and be yourself whilst still being able to negotiate your way through the relationship or friendship.

Love is fearless and brave and courageous and will stand firm in the face of cruelty and unkindness. It will fight with you, not against you, it will be there if you fall or fail or feel utterly bereft and distraught and broken. It will say 'no' when it has to and say 'yes' the rest of the time.

Love is gentle and kind and compassionate when we feel weak and vulnerable and lost. It does not try to take over or take advantage but just creates holding space while you regain equilibrium.

Love is wise and chooses not to be divided against others, but instead wishes to find harmony whilst not imposing on others.

Love seeks to give and nurture without taking credit for or taking away the achievements of the other.

Love is speaking out and taking risks with a friend or relationship when you think it should be said, even when they do not want to hear it, even when they move away from you as a result. You loved them more than you feared losing them and you will still be there if they walk away and then fall and turn to you once more.

Love means occasionally putting your needs second to the person you love.

In a good balanced relationship this will work so well because they will do the same thing for you so you are both blessed with being able to give your whole-hearted love and kindness and know you will receive in equal measure.

One you have learned the joy and liberating experience of giving your all to someone, to others even, then you will know a deep, deep loving joy.

Love means understanding the difference between needs and wants and learning to manage them yourself so that what the other gives to you is all bonus, excess. Your cup runneth over.

I like to think that my practice of mindfulness, which is pretty constant and daily, fills me up to the top with wellbeing and contentment so that I do not feel the need to hold on to anything inside myself, to keep anything back for myself, I am already overflowing and have plenty to share. So unless I am rejected or I feel the energy is not healthy as in above, then I am open and flowing in your direction. Love feeds me and nourishes and nurtures me so that I am available to others when they need me. For me that is what love means and what it feels like to love and be loved. Love and Happiness

Further thoughts on love and limits we place on ourselves

I was at a retreat workshop last week and a concept I have met before was represented to me in a way that made me rethink yet again my own life- I thought I would share with you all.

The basis is our self-limiting core values about our self and our place in life. What we allow our self to experience from the richness of what is available! The concept is that we allow ourselves a base line of love or success or happiness at any one time.

If our internal barometer looks like rising too high, we find ways to sabotage that experience until it comes into line again. If the barometer falls too low, we find ways to bring it up again. So it has real potential value on one hand but massive self-limiting issues on the other.

We limit our own access to love and happiness!

How mad is that, and yet it is true.

It also maintains parity with our other belief systems, our value systems, what we mean by happiness and success, what love actually feels like to us based on previous experience.

I still remember that line from the Marianne Williamson prayer 'Who are you not to be'.

Our deepest fear is not that we are inadequate. Our deepest fear is that we are powerful beyond measure. It is our light, not our darkness that most frightens us. We ask ourselves, who am I to be brilliant, gorgeous, talented, fabulous? Actually, who are you NOT to be? You are a child of God. Your playing small does not serve the world. There is nothing enlightened about shrinking so that other people won't feel insecure around you. We are all meant to shine, as children do. We were born to make manifest the glory of God that is within us. It's not just in some of us; it's in everyone. And as we let our own light shine, we unconsciously give other people permission to do the same. As we are liberated from our own fear, our presence automatically liberates others.

Wonderful inspirational words which still ring as true as they ever did because they are pure loving wisdom based on a deep truth.

But we sabotage ourselves so we keep within our narrow parameters of what we are personally allowed to have/ experience/access. We are only allowed this amount of happiness – this amount of love.

Even though we may crave for more love or happiness, we are not allowed to have it!

Because of my own childhood, (I know this is common to many though) I defensively and earnestly worked to want nothing, and then I had nothing to lose. But I had such joy in my true heart and such enthusiasm for life that I did want things and what is more I wanted my share of things. They came my way but I did not dare to value them too highly, to value myself too highly even, in case it was taken away from me and the pain of loss would be the greater for it.

It took me a long time to trust that I could rejoice in the love I was given. In spite of my various complications in life I am blessed by some very good friends and a lot of love. I also live in a comfortable place in the world, and I have learned a rich and wonderful load of teaching about love.

I have begun to wonder if that was what made being in the golden lagoon/ bliss state was so terrifying, it was too much, too nice, and my fear of having it taken away from me spoiled it for me, so that when it was taken away from me it was a relief.

I wonder if that was also why my earlier books were so well reviewed but did only sell moderately well, even though I was quoted by people like Deepak Chopra in online courses etc. But I was afraid after my first book – afraid that I could not repeat that level of writing again. I think my tension unconsciously sabotaged that too and in the end my relationship with my then publishers probably- when they got bought up, I was not taken into the new fold. Now they all need updating anyway.

I am in a wonderful marriage with someone who really gets me and is very affectionate and loving and yet I am still uncertain about its future from time to time and keep needing to check in with him. This is especially when things are going too well and then we hit a bump – internally I think 'oh right this is when it all falls apart on me again'.

These are just some of my versions of this 'upper limit, not allowed to have' stuff. You will have yours too; it may echo or be quite different. But as we are reminded above who are we not to be as happy as possible, as successful as possible in spiritually and emotionally healthy terms, as recognised for our gifts and accepted for our challenges as much as possible. It is time we loved ourselves enough to stop holding onto these self-limiting beliefs.

Money, wealth, abundance and lack

Although this is not an emotion per se it is based on emotional reactions and responses to the world and has some of the most complicated sets of emotions tangled up in it for us all.

Wealth and money are not the same thing.

I am wealthy beyond compare but I am not rich in money terms. I have health, life, happiness, deep joy, an interesting life, a fantastic marriage and soulmate. I have all my needs met and I don't actually want anything more than I have. I have contentment, but I am not self satisfied or smug about it, I know what it took me to get here and I value every last moment of it, every molecule, and every breath. That is my wealth. Money has no intrinsic value – everyone knows that – although there are many who appear not to, or to forget it. For them money is meaningful and represents something about them that makes them feel strong or proud or substantial in some way.

This is of course an illusion. It is only in their minds, our minds, your mind. That is not healthy or stable emotionally as a position in life and leads to always needing propping up. Celebrity status is a classic example of this approach to life. It is ultimately a very vulnerable position, but we all succumb to it at times. The more we all believe this system of wealth accumulation and showing off what you have, buying into the rhetoric, the more powerful the rich believe they are. In fact they just all feel entitled and are often very insecure.

There is a whole system of media and marketing to promote this approach to life and it is all based on making us unhappy and poorer so others can get richer.

BUT there is a far greater form of power than this and it is available for free and to all of us.

In fact those who seek power through money are going to be far less likely to find that power because they are looking in all the wrong places.

I am often asked about success and challenge the meaning of the word. What does success mean to you? As you read this you may think it is a trick question but it really is not at all. It is very straightforward - real power and real success can only be found internally, when you stop looking for them on the outside of yourself and instead find them on the inside. Power should never be power over other things or beings- that is not actually real power – that is domination. Real power is the power to create change for the common good, to make circumstances improve for the many.

Money is not power

Money is not status

Money is not love

Money is not success

Money is not wealth.

If you think it is then you have bought into the illusion. It's a very powerful one because so many people do believe in it. That might make it appear more real; the power of numbers, but it is still an illusion.

Money creates unhappiness, greed, lack mentality

Money creates poverty

- Poverty of compassion
- Poverty of love and sharing and caring and equality and justice and kindness and all the other things that help make life feel really skin tinglingly good to be living.

So what are abundance, wealth, and well being, apart from not being money?

The basics in life, which are essential to us all, must be available for wellbeing. That is a given, a basic human right. On an abundance mentality planet, that would be applied to all living beings. On this planet dominated by lack mentality, many do not have the dignity of a basic level of wealth so that they can live life well and contribute their talents and skills to the greater good. Decent health, food, clothing, shelter, and safety too. These are such simple things but for many people they are not available and that is because of the illusion of money and the great god 'Profit', otherwise known as Mammon, in the bible, the very thing we are warned not to worship is now the most popular unofficial god on the planet.

Beyond those basic survival needs we do not need anything else and everything else easily becomes a burden. I have more than those basics myself and I know they are both a privilege and a burden. That burden is upon others as much as it is upon us as a couple. A burden we are attached to because we no longer trust our country and society to care for us as we increasingly age. That should never be a concern for anyone. If anyone is vulnerable, they should be cared for as part of the human collective.

So much of human society is increasingly unequal and lacking compassion and concern for those who are vulnerable. You see I only need to plan for my elderly years because I cannot trust that the care will be there for me when I might need it. And that is the problem, this lack of equality means people feel insecure, which in turn creates more lack thinking because that is the self-perpetuating reality. I plan but I also trust in equal measure.

How do we turn this around?

The idea that if we have more makes us somehow safer or better or more successful people is the huge hole in human thinking. Turn it around!

If we disrespected everyone who had more than they actually needed and would not share more equally.

If society really poured scorn on extreme wealth and refused to service it, do you think the money would still matter so much?

If we scorned and spurned them instead of reading about them in celebrity magazines!

If instead we were only fascinated by the lives of those who have little enough beyond the basics, and how amazing these people are – if we gave them our attention and curiosity and tried to emulate them instead of those with shiny baubles which are the trappings of the great mental sickness called 'being rich'. If we redefined 'rich' as greed – a sign you are morally bankrupt – a sign you are corrupt and selfish and needy and unkind. Hollow people who need money to pretend they are something special. How attractive would 'rich' be in terms of external trappings?

Those with true skill can still be praised for that skill, but not expect the skill brings wealth with it, just respect, honour, kindness, and the chance to serve others more often. You get my drift.

So what does money give you in reality – just an illusion that so many people buy into and thus make it more attractive and more concrete, but still not real? Change the perception and it vanishes.

The effects of not having enough don't disappear, they are all too real for those living like that, yet they are often the freest happiest people. Zen master Thich Nhat Hanh has never held any personal money whatsoever, but he has done amazing things, built communities, stood up for peace, taught his wisdom to millions. It is possible. He is a Zen monk.

So, on a simple, normal person level how do we work towards this approach to life?

The key is gratitude for what you have rather than wanting more always, rejecting the influence of marketing and consumerism will make you happier, healthier, less stressed, and freer.

For me money is now just a tool with which to create change.

I want to live in a world which is not flat in equality because people are not the same – but one which is fair for all, that we all have the basics at least guaranteed for all, so there is no sense of competition for the resources- there is enough for all.

Change the ideology about money and you really do change the world for the better, everybody is richer in things that matter, which are real and not illusions, and no one wants 'more' because they have enough.

Aberrations can be contained easily enough and re-educated with gentleness and kindness and all will be taken care of. If wealth loses more than it gives then it will no longer be something that people seek, it will no longer be a symbol of success or be attractive.

I wonder what that might feel like for everyone. Just imagine feeling secure, valued, appreciated, and equal. Wow.

Narcissism

Narcissism is a nasty little problem, as Gollum would say. But it is one that we all have to some degree or another. It is more a state of mind, or even a mental health issue, but it is relevant to happiness and especially in my life.

Never mind the gorgeous young man who falls in love with his own image in the water and was transfixed. That is just self - image love and mirror gazing, which we all do, more often than not to re-assure ourselves that we look presentable to others. It is more a sign of insecurity.

Gollum's character is more like the personality disorder version of narcissism, just that they are usually much more convincing on the charm and less ugly. In other words quite plausible to those unwary enough or unfamiliar enough not to recognise it.

True narcissism is far more insidious than even Gollum though. It is ultimately potentially damaging / destructive to both the narcissist and anyone who comes into close or intimate contact with them. At arm's length they are more harmless and can be very entertaining. As soon as you have an emotional involvement you are likely to be in trouble, because that is when the games begin.

Narcissism has several varieties in its catalogue.

Grandiose narcissism - attention seeking - look at me - don't listen to anybody else it is all about me.

Malignant - as above but really intentionally nasty with it and often doing really bad things- almost a little psychopathic – cheat steal etc lie hurt- school bully type.

Covert – secret – butter wouldn't melt – put upon victim, still grandiose about how great they are but not recognised by others – may seem like depression but doesn't get better – woe is me, hyper sensitive to criticism – cold and distant if rejected. World doesn't get their greatness.

Stealth – every day is 'woe is me' – nice you got that thing - lucky for you - not so easy for me - check out how much of a victim they are and how much they say they want to change but don't – don't take responsibility – 'not my fault, everybody else made me do it'.

Communal narcissist – 'off to feed homeless today' – all about them – often very patronising in their sympathy – give good first impressions and often dress well but cannot give back in reality – lack of empathy and compassion, validation for all their good works needed, look how good **I am**!!!!!

We can all embody a little of this but how far it gets is how much of a problem it is and recognising it in one's self is the first way of knowing you are not a narcissist.

This is a topic that holds enormous significance for me. First of all I admit I have had some narcissistic tendencies in the past – through my historical deep insecurity and depression issues. These are the roots of narcissism. You will never find a truly self accepting individual who is narcissistic. Self acceptance means you stop worrying about yourself and get on with living and loving others.

Narcissism is always based on a deeply damaged sense of 'self' and 'other'. I have now developed enough skill in mindfulness and enough self-acceptance to be a great deal less narcissistic and it feels a whole load better.

My experiences of narcissistic others include parental, sexual partners and a variety of relationships, friendships, clients.

They would never have told me they had NPD but they were the ones for whom it is always everyone else's fault and thus they never made progress.

Generally I would say that if you are emotionally stable you would not get involved with a narcissist in the first place, because they feed from insecurities and vulnerabilities, using them as weapons against you, once they have won you over by being the most amazing partner/ friend you could ever imagine meeting. But when you are born to one you have no choice and you are doomed until you learn to truly break free.

A narcissist can be very compelling and addictive though, as the film about Liberace shows so well in Behind the Candelabra.

It is the selfish, self-centered, 'all about me' ego which demands its share, its turn, its rights, and dwells in the shadow of fear, regardless of the damage done to others, or how much hurt is caused generally to others.

I chose to discuss ego and ego issues through the vehicle of narcissism as well because in extremis ego is a serious personality problem called narcissistic personality disorder and rather a lot of people have it.

It is sad for them because inside they are a power-hungry ghost of a person with no real love or emotional connection with anyone or anything. They are locked into a prison of themselves and that is all they can perceive. Everything else is there to pander to their insatiable needs.

NPD is beyond selfishness though. It is far more insidious and devious in its tactics to dominate and achieve its goals of feeding its own insecurity, which is a bottomless pit.

It is often highly damaging to those who get close to people with NPD, and will frequently create Bi-Polar type problems for children of NPD's, based on Gregory Bateson's analysis of the permanent double bind of never being able to get it right for a parent with NPD.

Always wanting and trying so hard to please them and rarely being able to do so, because the rules will change all the time.

It is not intended that you should succeed since it is the trying they want from you, not the outcome. Your effort is their locus of control and ownership.

Bateson and R.D. Laing both suggested families create most mental health issues. In my case my mother almost certainly had undiagnosed NPD, and probably PTSD. I had PTSD as a result of both Mum and Dad.   A narcissistic parent will train their child to be a feed for them from as early as possible, i.e. someone there exclusively to meet their needs. The child is never parented but is the caregiver for the parent in some way or another.

Narcissism has stalked me through my life one way or another. I lived with it in childhood in a particularly nasty version, with Mother showing distinct psychopathic undertones. I also developed a mild form of narcissistic behaviour, partly to survive and partly as learned behaviour. I could have got stuck in that too, just like many people are. But I was lucky; I had a deep inner tutor called my intuition which led me away from that deep dark mire. And it showed me why too.

For many decades I was unconsciously attracted to that energy. Something inside me still wanted, at a heart yearning level unconsciously, to heal things with my mum. Again I unconsciously found other NPD people to try and work with instead. It is kind of addictive too, the amazing attraction of all that positivity coming at you in the early stages, make you feel so alive and having such fun. Until it turns.

I have had to learn how to manage the attraction of that energy within myself but I also have huge compassion for all mixed up with it. I have both personally and vicariously seen what it is to live within NPD and it is a living hell of one sort or another.

I think I have now learned to deal with that energy appropriately and create good boundaries for myself from its damaging energy, but I am also sad that I have not been able to reach or help to change those who taught me these lessons. Perhaps they have more people to teach but I hope they all find inner peace and happiness at some time. Mother never did!

All I know is that it is ultimately very destructive and although some people with NPD can be great fun and very entertaining, you are only ok if you expect nothing in return from them. I learned that lesson the very hard way.

I gravitated towards these people without ever recognising that was what I was doing. I found them impressive, fascinating, charming, compelling even. It took me several tough experiences to recognise my own compliance in these devastations of my fragile sense of self. This eventually led me to realise there is no self, to accept who you are in a given moment is all that is required, nothing more than that. Who you are in a given moment is an utterly unique, a 'rarely if ever to be repeated moment' and the influences around you co- creating the 'you' in this moment are equally fleeting and impermanent.

I know I did not have NPD because I do change, hungrily wanting to do so, and I have an adult ADHD diagnosis which has very similar outlooks on life to milder cases of Autism Spectrum Disorder. I take things very literally, cannot abide tact (it's lying) and am direct and specific. Thus it can seem like I don't care about others. But I do and very deeply and probably more than I care about myself. Much of my self-absorption is about how to manage my ADHD and be better for other people.

Narcissism is so complex a disorder, and so deeply enmeshed within my own life that I decided to break with my usual model and use several quotes from distinguished others to make my points.

Here are some informed insights you might relate to or find interesting

"Narcissistic personality disorder is named for Narcissus, from Greek mythology, who fell in love with his own reflection. Freud used the term to describe persons who were self-absorbed, and psychoanalysts have focused on the narcissist's need to bolster his or her self-esteem through grandiose fantasy, exaggerated ambition, exhibitionism, and feelings of entitlement."

— Donald W. Black, DSM-5 Guidebook: The Essential Companion to the Diagnostic and Statistical Manual of Mental Disorders

A straightforward description with a medical / psychiatric basis. I like this, it sums it up although is very general and easily misses the finer details of true NPD. One thing I have noticed about people with NPD is that they are pathologically incapable of loving in any meaningful sense of the word. They want the status of you as a child/ partner/friend etc. They want to extract love from you and use you to gain their own ends. I knew someone who always used his daughter to gain favour and friendship, to make a good impression. He didn't trust himself to do this alone. Next, from one of my favourite authors on the topic of love.

"The main condition for the achievement of love is the overcoming of one's narcissism. The narcissistic orientation is one in which one experiences as real only that which exists within oneself, while the phenomena in the outside world have no reality in themselves, but are experienced only from the viewpoint of their being useful or dangerous to one. The opposite pole to narcissism is objectivity; it is the faculty to see other people and things AS THEY ARE, objectively, and to be able to separate this OBJECTIVE picture from a picture which is formed by one's desires and fears."

— Erich Fromm, The Art of Loving

My own experiences of NPD have been a total absence of actual love of any kind, starting with my mother, - she could adore people who met her needs but she had no objectivity, you were either on her side or her enemy. There was no middle ground, unless you ignored her and then she was just plain furious and condemnatory of that person for being so ignorant as to ignore her or deem her unimportant in their life.

"Narcissists are consumed with maintaining a shallow false self to others. They're emotionally crippled souls that are addicted to attention. Because of this they use a multitude of games, in order to receive adoration. Sadly, they are the most ungodly of God's creations because they don't show remorse for their actions, take steps to make amends or have empathy for others. They are morally bankrupt."

— Shannon L. Alder

One of the biggest problems for someone with NPD is that they cannot see beyond their own needs. They will feel very isolated and alone on the inside but pretend this isn't true to the world. No matter how much attention they receive, they are the hungry ghosts, the bottomless pits of emotional need. Once I was healed from those early influences, I stopped being overly self aware. Writing about my experiences, they all feel emotionally detached, as if they all happened to someone I once knew. My purpose for writing it all down is to help other people to recognise their own parallels and move forward on them. I use my story because it is so rich a vein to follow and mine for content, and I have my permission to say what I say. But it is my story too of course, my perspective, my experience. So I do not think it is absolute truth, just my own subjective truth.

One we get away from self and self needs- once we recognise that self is an empty concept, we can start to look more objectively at one's own behaviour, his or herstory, and generally view life through a different lens.

"The faculty to think objectively is REASON; *the emotional attitude behind reason is that of* HUMILITY. *To be objective, to use one's reason, is possible only if one has achieved an attitude of humility, if one has emerged from the dreams of omniscience and omnipotence which one has as a child. Love, being dependent on the relative absence of narcissism, requires the development of humility, objectivity and reason.*

I must try to see the difference between MY *picture of a person and his behaviour, as it is narcissistically distorted, and the person's reality as it exists regardless of my interests, needs and fears."*

— *Erich Fromm, The Art of Loving*

I have not always been able to do this but I am aware of that and try not to do it anymore. This is a clue that I am not NPD. Just in case you hadn't realised- being like my mother is, has been, and always will be, my greatest fear. My second greatest fear is having to be close to someone with NPD – it is too destructive.

I feel deeply sad for anybody who has NPD or anybody who grew up with an NPD parent. That latter is a nightmare that cannot be under-estimated. The outcomes of long-term mental health issues and damaged lives that flow out from that point are such a high price to pay for all concerned.

I used my mother's own tactics against her, to reject and keep her at arm's length, but also to reflect back to her how she was with me. That doesn't work with NPD. What is more, it wasn't kind but it was all I could do to keep her from destroying what was left of me.

She was afraid of me too as she knew I saw through her clearly, through her games, her self-pity, her anger and posturing and pretences to be someone with culture and breeding.

Despite this, by the time she died, I felt nothing but compassion for her but was unable to reach her as her defenses were so guarded against me and also she was by now taken over completely by her groomer, her best friend whom she regarded as her surrogate brother (she had two sisters) and her 'carer' in latter years.

The only person she trusted because he met her need to be adored and believed and loved, and there was enough money available to make that worth his while. So he was her back up when her going got tough because she knew that she had alienated her own children and grand-children. She wanted someone to feel sorry for her over this 'abandonment by her own children' and allow her to play the innocent victim, which she did to great aplomb and he took it and played it back to her so skillfully.

Narcissism is now an energy force that I can sense a mile off. I can see it in differing degrees in almost everyone but in some it is beyond the normal levels of self preservation which we all need, it is ruining their lives.

I am so lucky I did not get stuck in NPD, I could have done.

I escaped the narcissism vortex, the black hole of emptiness and hollowness, of deep inner loneliness and lack of trust.

I feel soo incredibly sad for those who are stranded there, it is a bleak place but there is nothing anybody can do for them until they realise it and work to come back from it. I think that is possible in some people but mostly it is a hopeless cause as it was with my own mother and their demise is a lonely and sad one.

> *"Realize that narcissists have an addiction disorder. They are strongly addicted to feeling significant. Like any addict they will do whatever it takes to get this feeling often. That is why they are manipulative and future fakers. They promise change, but can't deliver if it interferes with their addiction. That is why they secure back up supply."*
>
> *— Shannon L. Alder*

Orgasms

How the quest for an orgasm led me to happiness – really it did! But oh boy did it take me through a lot of bad stuff first.

Is sex just about Orgasms? Is an orgasm a measure of good sex? Is it just a natural physical release of tension and sexual energy brought on by certain activities? Or is it some unique energy exchange between two people who are truly connected spiritually/ emotionally and in a deep communication with each other?

This essay / account is the one I wish someone had given me to read when I was much younger and what I have subsequently learned as I grew older and older. What is a life without orgasms?

I disagree with my own first statement although I know some people think the number or size of their orgasms is something to celebrate; a statement of their sexual prowess. But in that case is masturbation something to celebrate when it is so solitary and can be a symbol of loneliness, or used as a statement of independence and self-reliance. These contradictory view-points show how complex this all is.

Now I know this could be controversial and I am fine about this. I am happy for people to disagree with me but I would say this is <u>my</u> relationship with the mystical orgasm in my life and thus my subjective and exclusively female experience. It is also about a specific time in human emotional and cultural sexual evolution. There are lessons to be taken from it nevertheless.

When I was growing into adolescence, western sexual attitudes were very confused, as they are still now of course, but more suppressed and oppressive than this current era.

Travelling the Alphabet Emotionally

By the time I reached puberty, as far as I was aware of, feminism hadn't really addressed female sexuality properly, let alone the idea of an actual equal relationship between men and women.

Yet contraception was being made freely available with the advent of the contraceptive pill. But there was no guidance for women to express how they felt or what they wanted from sex, just an assumption that the Pill made them more 'restriction free' and thus available to men. The two worst things were to be seen to be 'frigid' or to be 'loose'. The fear of unwanted pregnancy had now started to fade and sexually transmitted disease / AIDS had not yet hit the headlines.

So let me start at my beginning. My first awareness of feelings that I now understand are sexual arousal was just after puberty, mostly in dreams. I had very powerful dreams that there was a mystical being, this lover, waiting somewhere for me. He would arrive at some point in my life. I would actually meet this dream lover. He was strong and slim and kind and had a soft voice and took great care of my body and gave me great pleasure. It felt as if I already really deeply knew this man, knew his energy, knew his deepest spiritual core, his hidden and true nature, but not yet. The knowledge of him left me aroused and confused. I had no-one to trust in my life, so no-one to share my experiences with.

I didn't learn how to or even know about the concept of self-relief or masturbation, so I was left with these unfulfilled arousal feelings which I then coped with by suppressing, as I'd learned to do with all confusing and conflicted emotional states. I certainly couldn't talk to anyone about it. At home there was a very oppressive emotional regime, no open communication, just a list of 'forbiddens' to even talk about, let alone explore. At school I couldn't bear to show my innocence or ignorance, let alone my inner world of dreams and hopes and mystical experiences.

Sex knowledge was just mechanics and something to be talked about, giggled over, wondered about and according to adults – avoided.

It was a source of curiosity and shame, about childish decisions that we would make when the time came and which we would never understand how little control we may have over those times.

Contrast this with my mother's abusive approach to sexual education at home, making a point of showing me my father's semen stained bed-sheets as evidence of how cruel he was because he wouldn't touch her any more. I was about thirteen at that time.

And combine this with those powerful feelings in my body which were taking on a force of their own as I went through puberty into adolescence and young adulthood.

I was utterly lost and confused. How on earth was I supposed to know how to deal with this situation? No one ever explained what kind of feelings you might grow into or how to cope with them, or what they even meant. I believe this is still the case for too many young people, and it is a terrible flaw in our whole attitude towards sexuality.

I was also emotionally frozen and terrorised still at this point. Nevertheless physical and sexual maturity beckons to us all, whatever our circumstances and readiness for them.

My first overt sexual encounter was in Austria and again I felt that inexplicable feeling of arousal through the physicality of dancing with someone, but nothing more. More suppression of awakening desires followed but left me feeling empty and aching and longing and all the other confusing feelings that come with unrequited arousal.

Some year or so later, in south London, I met someone at a dance and agreed to meet up the following afternoon. I was so naive and inexperienced, but also hopeful that someone might just like me.

Perhaps I was about to achieve that longed for status – to have a boyfriend!

So when he started to have sex with me, without asking, or without me really knowing what was happening – I just froze. His parents came home and their presence stopped it all and I left. To this day nearly fifty years later on I still don't really know what happened. I think my body protected me, didn't let him enter me, but I was swollen and sore for the next few days. I thought I had been raped but I just didn't know. I did say 'no' but was it my fault, had I not said no loudly enough, had I given mixed messages?

As I sit here typing this out I realise how long it has taken for me to speak openly about what actually happened. I went to stay at a friends' house that night and she was very kind to me, then the following Monday at school I pretended that I didn't care about it and just turned it into a laugh. As far as I was concerned, I was no longer a virgin, although technically I think I almost certainly still was.

My next encounter with sex was following the realisation that my currency as 'girlfriend material' was based only on my willingness to have sex. I had been set up with a friend of a friend and he assumed that at the end of the evening I would have sex with him. I turned him down and was told a few days later by a girlfriend in that group that I had indeed had sex with him. I was so desperate for inclusiveness that I then agreed to see him again and that was that.

I was expected to give him sex a few times a week in return for him putting his arm round my neck when we walked down the street. That was it. I actually did get slightly fond of him for a while, then mind-bogglingly bored and stopped seeing him. I don't think I ever experienced even a shallow level of arousal though, I was a commodity for him sexually and he was a commodity for me status wise – I had a boyfriend.

Thereafter I continued to allow men to have sex with me, thinking that at some point I would feel something, pretending with all the bravado of that age that I did like sex and gradually being more and more damaged by this roundabout of use. I never got anything from it, no arousal and definitely no orgasm, I read cosmopolitan articles about orgasms and wondered what was wrong with me. I was so scared of being called a prick tease or frigid so I acted out like it was all fine and I was on board with this. I even tried to pretend that I was in control and this was how I saw myself. Control based on suppression is not control though, it is abuse survival, and that is what I was doing, barely surviving inside.

I don't blame anybody and don't accuse them of rape, but in reality it was, because no one ever checked to make sure I was ok. In today's frames of reference I realise it was all rape rape rape. I say this for one simple reason. I didn't know that I had the right to say, 'no I don't like this'.

My father had used my body to take out his violent anger with my mother and I didn't know how to stop other men using me in a similar way, sexually, emotionally and occasionally with physical violence, just like my Dad had done. This pattern continued for many years afterwards.

By the age of seventeen I felt worthless to a much higher level than my parents had managed to create, because I had shown myself that they were right by acknowledging the rest of the world also saw me like this. I had been suicidal more or less for the previous three or more years and I hit a real low. I became bulimic, overweight, self-harming by using pumice to try and scrape all the skin from my body, as if I wanted to get out of my skin and cleanse myself of it all.

Also I wanted to break free of that protective frozen shell but I couldn't even begin to identify that yearning at that stage. Somewhere inside I wanted someone to recognise who I was, someone with whom I could fully connect.

Travelling the Alphabet Emotionally

Then just before I was eighteen, I met my first husband and he was, and still is, a nice man, so I stuck with him for thirteen years even though we were emotionally and intellectually about as incompatible as I can imagine. We were both lonely and felt worthless, and for a while we filled that need for 'someone to want us' in each other. My step-mother more or less pushed me onto him, even when I showed and felt misgivings about the quality of our relationship, she more or less said 'don't look a gift horse in the mouth', or 'be grateful for what you get offered'. I took the hint and moved in with him.

We got married after two years dating and then living together. I did my best to be happy and was now so good at conning myself that I did a good job of it too. We did have fun sometimes. We did travel a little and talk sometimes. I think I did love him properly for a while but it never felt reciprocated, like there was an energy feeler out there looking for something to connect with and it couldn't find a connection, so eventually it withdrew. In many ways this also broke my heart, I had so wanted this to be right for us forever, but it just didn't have legs.

We did go out and have friends and a sort of social life. But he was 'pipe and slippers married' and I was drowning in stagnation and duty and routine. I wanted and needed more, more life stimulation, more emotional connection, more intellectual sharing and development. I tried and tried to find this in our relationship but it wasn't ever there.

I got ill a couple of times, once with pancreatitis and once with an ectopic pregnancy. I was told that I might not be able to have children, so suddenly that became a priority even though we had never spoken of this before at all in our relationship.

Sex was about getting pregnant for the next two years or so.

And yet I didn't want to get pregnant.

I wanted it to happen by accident.

It was too big a decision to take, even though we were married and everyone expects you to have children, and there was some pressure for that on one side, of aspirational grand-parenting at least.

But then it was taking a long time to happen. I had no idea of these layers of turmoil going on inside me at that time, but I can see them now on reflection.

We had two sons some six and eight years after marriage. Giving birth was the first time I felt the true emotional side-effects of oxytocin, that miracle neurotransmitter which helps you to bond to people. My darling little boys were the people who started to melt that frozen core inside me and I started to have proper feelings. Unfortunately I found the difference between real feelings and those I had been telling myself I should have, based on duty and loyalty and commitment. Wow what a difference, I could pretend no longer.

I discovered that I had the ability to have orgasms if I wasn't having sex, through reading literature which included sexual scenes, I don't mean cliterature, I mean ordinary books that just included sex as part of the story. I sometimes managed an orgasm during actual sex but they were a struggle and yet on my own I could flow quickly and easily. I developed a solitary practice, but eventually I was so deeply angry with that lonely reality that I couldn't manage even that any more.

By then there was no companionship in our marriage either and I couldn't convince myself that I was happy any longer. I also started to find other men very attractive again, a sure sign something was changing in me.

The marriage broke up and we both moved on.

We were both hurt but I closed my shell so I probably didn't show it much at all. It was how I survived life generally anyway; this was just another one of those.

I met new men but nothing lasted for that long.

Travelling the Alphabet Emotionally

Some of the sex was good in terms of orgasms, some was emotionally abusive/NPD but I was too damaged to notice the difference in those days. I often faked orgasms to please men with fragile self-esteems and no real interest in my well-being. I think without intending to be I became quite ruthless in trying to get what I wanted but also vulnerable and still pretty frozen and deeply afraid of all men, although I'd not yet fully realised that dimension of it.

The penultimate relationship I had lasted a little over five very trying years and it really got nasty for me at the end, NPD games, it all left me frozen up again, in early stages of PTSD as I now recognise it to be.

I was 'garlic and silver crosses' towards all men who thought of anything more than just friendship, and not even that close a friendship please. I thought that was how it would be for me. Some twenty-seven years later I had forgotten how the man in my dreams had ever been visiting me regularly at night and leaving me feeling so wonderfully fulfilled and loved, even though nothing had happened, I hadn't even masturbated.

 Then I met my second husband. There was something different about him, he was quiet and gentle. We met one year at Cambridge Folk Festival and nothing developed so we both went back the following year hoping to meet again. We did. And that was it really. We talked non-stop for the whole time, he took my phone number and rang me and I went down to see him that weekend. We talked more and again remained quite chaste and respectful of our personal physical boundaries. And then we kissed and started talking in a whole new way.

Suddenly there it was, that recognition. I felt as if I had just taken the elevator to the basement several layers of consciousness below that which I thought was all that existed. We talked on whole new levels. Then we kissed and held each other and eventually managed to pluck up the confidence to go to bed.

It was as if neither of us had ever had sex before. We had of course - we were both parents and that is a bit of a giveaway. But I suddenly knew the difference between having sex and making love. There was no performance needed, no techniques necessary. This was him, this was exactly the man I knew when I was fifteen, he smelt, sounded and felt exactly like I remembered him and I wondered how I'd managed to forget I was looking for him.

But perhaps I hadn't forgotten at a deeper level, my soul was looking for its mate and that was why all those other relationships had never been able to last. It wasn't me just fulfilling my mother's prophesy that no one would like me once they got to know me. Because here was this mystical union I had read about and thought not possible. Orgasms took on another whole level of both irrelevance and importance at the same time. It no longer mattered if they did or did not happen but when they did it felt as if we had melted into one being.

We could talk about it all, and more importantly laugh about it all. It took us both time, of course, as we had both been damaged by previous relationships, but that didn't matter either. We were together now and we took our time to explore everything possible with each other. We gave each other the freedom to be who we each really were inside, those core beings which we had both hidden away in childhood for safe keeping and could now bring out and share with complete freedom and acceptance. We both prefer gentleness and tenderness and taking time. Neither of us wanted to 'achieve' anything.

It possibly helps that we were both older by then and our bodies were less driven as they are in youth, but it felt so free and lovely and honest and intimate and just plain right.

So the letter I would write to myself back then would include the following points:

Travelling the Alphabet Emotionally

Don't feel ashamed of any journey you take through life, you never know where it will lead you and perhaps you need to have certain experiences to really appreciate others that come along later. Never judge the lesson. Only appreciate the outcomes.

Don't let other people use you and make you feel like somehow you owed it to them but also are now worthless to them.

Don't let other people put you down for exploring and trying to find meaning and authenticity in your life, you often need to go through what it is not before you find what it is, both your own and other people's.

Let the person you love show you who they are and never project onto them your expectations which you will then use to judge them through and hurt them and destroy any potential you might have for happy relationships.

Make sure they do the same thing for you though.

Understand that the body and person who was abused or used is not who you are now, that body has long since passed into an alternative existence. There is probably not a cell alive in me now that pre-dates meeting my soulmate, so which body was it that was abused in such ways.

Honour your own body, not as a commodity to be used to attract others or gain what you need inside, but as a beautiful home for your own spirit.

Know that true love cannot be found that easily and needs time and effort to work to develop it.

I met my soul mate but it has not been an easy journey to reach over twenty years of increasingly harmonious and happy intimate closeness. We both had to work hard on ourselves to learn how to be the best person we could for each other without ever selling out for ourselves.

The trouble is that back then I would have read this letter maybe, I would probably not have understood or related or properly understood at all, and I probably would not have been able to act upon it.

An orgasm is not worth the price if it is not part of love and it is not a real orgasm until you have had the complete shared energy connection.

It is a shadow of its potential but it could spoil the whole possibility of sacred sexual connection for you into the future if you waste this gift.

The point is that we are all doing the best we can with what we know. It is most often the very bad experiences which push us towards the light if we let them, but we have to be ready for that to happen in the first place. I had to find oxytocin and love from giving birth before I realised that almost all I had experienced up until then was not love, it was mutual dependency, ownership and control, and many other things but none of them really love. Not as I now know it at least. I had to reconstruct my parental relationships with other people before I recognised this was what I was doing and then change that pattern. I had to learn to listen to the yearnings of my heart before I knew what I was looking for and I had to learn to value what I have and not always be looking for what was out there for me to move onto next.

In a sense the story of my life is one of how the quest for the orgasm led me to find true love and happiness, how it led me through dark times so that I would recognise the light, and also to break open the shell that the little girl I used to be constructed around herself to protect herself from the abuse she was suffering and without which she would not have made it through alive or sane.

Thank you, sacred orgasms, for your divine wisdom.

The Past

The past is again not exactly an emotion but it contains emotional recollections - a place where we can store very deep emotional issues. Our relationship with the past is often central to our emotional healing. It is extremely complex and can appear contradictory.

So many people are haunted by the past, by the baggage they carry from it, by the hurts. They believe they have a good memory of the past, but do they? Ask yourself this

Are you still afraid of that toothache you had when you were two yrs. old and cutting new teeth? NO!

Can you even remember that pain?

Can you remember that joy from the first time you felt a flower or grass or sunshine?

Can you remember your first cuddle?

These are all things that happened to us in the past but we probably don't remember them, or not many of them. This suggests your memory isn't that accurate or solid at all.

We say we remember the past but we do not. We rehearse the bits we choose to cling onto. Sometimes a hazy flicker of a shadow will come into view and remind us of an old memory but usually they are vague and far distant- from another time, another you. And so, all true memories are this and nothing more than this, a shadow, a hint. Unless you rehearse them, they will fade.

Or do they?

Trauma leaves a deeper mark. It penetrates our bodies and weaves its energy into the fabric of our being at cellular level. It can stay there undetected for some time, until something releases this cellular memory and then the trauma re- emerges.

This is not rehearsed. This is as it is, as it was, relived.

Re-membered, as in put back together in its entirety of moment by moment experience, as you lived it, in full technicolour nightmare recall, sometimes with amplified sounds effects too. This is memory trapped by the amygdale and hippocampus, and not released to move on through the cortex and allowed to fade. This results in PTSD and requires special treatment to heal.

But generally you can leave the past behind you if you let it go—or quite a lot of it anyway. It is just a fiction, a memory, a perceptual position you or someone else once took about a sequence of events. It is not real anymore, so leave behind as much as you want to.

What does your story allow to you release, to forget? All the good bits. All the bits that do not fit your version of events. Do you remember the first time you saw a butterfly and what joy that felt, what amazement at such visual beauty and fragility?

What if your present ego demands that this story be kept alive and re-iterated endlessly as so-called memory?

What you can't get away from is what is inside you. You can never escape anything until you release it.

Your anger, your fear, your bitterness, your shame and guilt. But they are not the past, they are just labels we hang on it. Annotations for our story so that we are the hero, or the victim. Others are lesser beings, always, lesser players in our narrative or else so large that they are monsters, super-humans upon which we place too much responsibility for our own story.

I have been incredibly happily re-married for several years now but before that not so lucky. I don't relate to that person any more though. Even the person who made her marriage vows in 2000 is not the same body, not the same bones, not the same cells, not the same age, not the same thoughts, not the same experiences, not the same life paradigms.

Each day I renew my marriage vows; to make sure they are up to date and present moment real, not ever a memory, never the past.

The past is always going and the future always coming quickly towards me, but the spaciousness of now is endless and illuminated brightly.

The past is a strange and distant land, but one we think we are familiar with. We can change that paradigm.

The past is a rich resource for learning from, and then releasing. Never avoid or run from it, it is very sticky and will undercut you forever if you do not ace up to it, but it is not a place to dwell in either.

My mother lived totally in the past, and she was such an unhappy person. My father ran away from it.

Peacefulness, inner peace, deep peace.

Complete inner peace is that very rare thing- some venerable old masters at meditation may have it but most of us do not.

I don't - but I have a lot more of it than I used to have. That is lovely.

I understand what is it though, having glimpsed it in various forms through bliss, meditation, making love, sleep, walking along the beach in the evenings with my soul-mate, sitting watching sunsets, travelling even, amongst many truly peaceful times. Often it is just stopping my mind and taking a breath.

Peace means no conflict. No inner conflict, no outer conflict either. It means being at one with the world and thus it incorporates many other qualities and attributes which combine to create peace. It is a highly skilful emotional level to reach. It means being fully present in the now, the moment in which you are experiencing the peace, when nothing else exists. It means that externally, at least for the moment, you are not in demand or being confronted with sadness in your life, with challenges that feel overwhelming. But that is the only external influence over your inner peace.

Internally it means you have mastered a few key life skills, or are at least on the way to mastering them.

Peace comes from acceptance that you are not the all powerful being your ego likes to think you are.

Peace comes from allowing your-self to be human, and to have compassion for that humanness with its tendency to mess up sometimes.

'It's ok, be at peace with your messy-up-ness.'

Peace comes from loving the life you actually have right now, not wanting anything different yet being open to change happening – because it will change, and fearing that will remove your inner peace without stopping change happening.

Peace comes from gratitude for the life you have lived, for all of it, ups and downs alike, for embracing your whole life journey to date and being open to what might develop out of this moment.

Peace means appreciating the people in your life for exactly who they are, warts 'n all, for all they show you – love or challenges – that's their gift.

Peace comes from not wanting to change the world but quietly knowing you can work towards making it a better place for at least a few people each day, probably in ways you do not even know about.

Peace comes from knowing you have done your best in all that you faced today, which is all anyone can do, but accepting and acknowledging that.

Peace comes from mastering your thoughts and editing them for constructive helpful ones to spend time with and allowing unhelpful negative ones to dissipate. We all need feedback and constructive criticism, but we don't ever need decimation.

Peace comes from giving your best to those around who love you the most and give you their best also.

Peace comes from doing what is in your heart, doing what is dear to your value system and not allowing others to deter you, even if that may cause conflict for them. Know that it is not your conflict.

Peace comes from the path of mindfulness and meditation, learning to focus the mind and train it to see clearly what is real and what is true and to lose all false perceptions.

Peace comes from experiencing the inter-connectedness of all life and feeling part of it to your core. From knowing that although you are always evolving, exactly as you are right now is exactly how you are meant to be.

Praise and criticism

Neither praise nor criticism are totally positive in the long run, because they are external to you and thus make you dependent on other people's views of you to help you feel better or worse, i.e. turn you into a praise junkie or highly self critical. They are also both open to abuse.

Praise is only worth something if you know that it is totally sincere and has no hidden agenda. But often people use it like 'I am only praising you so that you owe me/ praise me back' or it can turn you into praise dependency and that will make you vulnerable to coercion to do anything to 'get praise', and thus never sincere.

On the other hand, praise can be helpful and allow you to see the good in yourself also when you hold yourself in poor regard. Some people have great difficulty accepting praise that is meant genuinely. For decades this was true of me. I never trusted it, having watched my mother in action and how easily people fell for her games. I heard what she said about them behind their backs you see, and knew she was disingenuous, and visa versa. If I ever got anything akin to praise from her, it also felt more like pressure to perform further, coercive, rather than pleasure in what I had just done, genuine praise.

It doesn't matter how much praise you give, if there is coercion in it, it is just as damaging as critical comments.

Criticism can be helpful if it is received lovingly as feedback and not as a condemnation of you as a person which is so often how it is delivered.

In this latter case welcome it for the feedback and take the sting out of it, dis-empower its negativity and empower yourself simultaneously.

You will be surprised at the effects it has on those who want to use criticism to make you feel bad about yourself when you embrace their comments in a way that keeps you in control.

Withholding feedback can be another form of manipulative game playing designed to make you feel bad. It is often the basis for relationship failures. How can you change something you don't know?

Feedback is crucial to our positive development. We need to know what it is that we get wrong. So if someone withholds feedback, they are keeping you in 'being wrong' mode which makes them feel superior and 'better than', a particularly insidious form of judging others. This is another example of harmful ego games - using praise/criticism to manipulate it and to keep others in the place where they can be made use of for another's needs.

If on receiving criticism, you remain in victim mode and place them in 'being wrong for being unkind' mode, it can never help any relationship to thrive positively.

Kind feedback is loving and helpful but you may not want to hear it. That is up to you how you discern the difference. As I have just said - you can use both - beneficially - for yourself of course and dis-empower the unkind versions by 'thanking them for the insight and you will consider it in your own time'.

 I remember once in later years when my mother still tried to play her unkind power games with me. She told me how unattractive I was and I just looked at her and suggested her opinion no longer mattered to me. I and others disagreed with her and maybe she was wrong. The look of fury and disempowerment on her face said it all.

She had wanted to hurt me and failed.

I had taken back control.

I was not unkind, just stated the fact and moved on.

It is better to create your own value system and to work to that, know your own truths, improving on your performance daily if you can and being your own manager without criticism or praise, just a progress report.

Meditation and mindfulness help us enormously to develop a self examination approach to life. That is one of their main purposes and values, the ability to recognise and change our expressions of less helpful qualities and turn them into positive ones.

Praise should mean more like give thanks to, i.e. praise be the lord or something like that. Praise for something well done that enables or supports others, encouragement for a skill being mastered etc.

Personal praise risks giving people the wrong idea about them self, praise gets hijacked by the ego and turns into 'I am something great'. This immediately creates imbalances in self importance, especially too much praise of the wrong kind i.e. eliciting approval in childhood.

Too much praise of the wrong kind can lead to NPD. Or it puts someone on a pedestal which is a very uncomfortable place to be and almost always they will want to fall off to get away from the pressure or else they will get pushed off, or become utterly narcissistic - then you won't get them off anyway.

So handle both praise and criticism with care, they are powerful tools and can be so helpful but so damaging too. And consider how much praise or criticism you level at yourself too, are you being fair here???

I have never praised myself ever- I think I am unable to do so, but I can accept myself which is probably more emotionally healthy. I have however learned to stop punishing myself for messing up sometimes, for having ADHD, for having PTSD, for not being perfect. It is ok to be me, as long as I continually re-evaluate that 'me'.

Prejudgments and Prejudice

This is a topic that I feel very strongly about but am not going to pretend that I haven't also been guilty of too, in the past. I try harder nowadays. It is only by having fallen into that trap myself and also been on the receiving end of it that I can actually write with honesty and insight from both perspectives, which I will attempt to do here.

All pre-judgments are mistaken beliefs about some other when you haven't even bothered to get to know them properly in the first place. The trouble is it might be based on some element of truth, just not all of it, and thus appears to be valid. That is the first mistake. Once the prejudgment becomes locked into place in your mind, it then becomes a prejudice, which is far more unshakeable.

The kinds of people who fall into the receiving end of this general human behaviour are, all women, men and women of any colour – depending on where you are in the world, physically or mentally disabled, mentally ill, cognitively disadvantaged, sexually diverse, divorced, married, single, gender conflicted male female or androgen, poor, addicted, older or elderly.

I am not afraid of black people for instance but I am afraid of their much-justified anger at how they are mistreated collectively in UK. I have felt fear walking down a predominantly black street in this town where I once lived and was born, which I did not feel with people of the same colour in African, Asian or South American countries. Do they see me as a perpetrator, which I am by default as a white person, but about which I am powerless to make the change on my own – much as I want to? They perhaps prejudge me as white and thus oppressor or racially prejudiced. I am not, I am just afraid of anger – that is my PTSD.

So who have I missed off the list?

And now think what percentage of the world's population this amounts to.

So that is pretty much all of us.

I even put white men into this category since they are also subject to prejudice from other groups because of their perceived privilege.

So now it is all of us.

However those prejudgments are seriously deleterious to the target groups they refer to – again I make no distinction here which group is most hurt, but we all suffer as a result.

This is the point I want to make the most strongly – all of humanity suffers as a result of these pre-judgements- all – without fail – even if they do not directly notice it- it is still there.

I want the human race to benefit from me as much as I want to benefit from the human race.

On my travels through life and through my childhood I was taught to look down on certain categories of people as lesser than us as a family. In fact talking to a dear cousin recently - she confessed she had once been also fooled into thinking our family was something special, so I know it is not just me.

Some of us may have done all sorts of things but scratch a little deeper and you find out how much we really are not in any way special. In fact it is that real truth – yep - we are not that great after all - which makes us insecure in our family and individual value, and thus needing to assert our superiority to make ourselves feel better.

I know the family story and where this deeper level of worthlessness comes from, generations back, but the over-compensation is just as damaging to future generations and has its repercussions still. Actually accepting yourself for whom and what you are is a far more stable, non-comparative approach.

Now take other alternatives like mental health or disability issues. I have two of these and they run through my family as they are both passed on through certain types of abusive behaviour and also genetically. Take the dyslexia, dyspraxia, dysgraphia, dyscalculia family and their close cousins ADHD and Autism spectrum. You would not believe how many comments fly about that they cannot be from this side of the family or that side of the family. 'That would mean we have a defective gene and that threatens our superiority issues'. Well yes, we do have that gene and it runs through on all sides. So perhaps more than one branch has it too! I ask you though – does it really matter?

CAN'T WE ALL JUST BE WHO WE ARE, AS WE ARE, AND THAT IS ENOUGH.

I shall now use the word 'difference' to include all conditions that could be included in the 'prejudice against' brackets

The prejudgment here is that it is bad to have this difference. The emotionally healthy attitude would be - wow if they can do this instead that is amazing. Because that is the point, with all differences, there are wonderful compensations, which should be celebrated. So how often do we hear about them?

NO! - they are seen as problems by people who are not in that category, who – just like my family – are somehow convinced of their lower value and wants to find someone else further down even than them to feel better than. It is all comparative – and all a huge mistake in thinking and attitude, aided and abetted by the language used.

Difficult to manage, causes problems, require special consideration, can be challenging, is too financially state dependent, and doesn't offer anything back to society.

Some of the people who caused me most problems have been well intentioned people who are not in those categories specified above, i.e. are no kind of social psychological emotional problem at all.

But their ignorance has been devastating to me and I know this is a common experience.

If I take ADHD as my example, I recently 'came out' to a community of people that I have ADHD and am recovering from PTSD. Since then I have been variously told that members don't believe ADHD exists or that I am too challenging for them to cope with.

No I Am Not – it is their lack of openness and judgements that creates any challenge and they are not my issue. I am what I am and they are what each of them are, individually. We all bring challenges to each other and we can all grow and learn through that.

I did a little survey on Quora recently about the experiences people with ADHD have had regarding discipline as a child and in education, and what the long-term outcomes of those experiences have been. Out of the many responses I received only one said they had had a good supportive family background which has enabled them to learn to manage their ADHD disadvantages and make the most of the benefits. A parent who can nurture and enable their child is the most precious experience and sadly it is not that common. All the other responses talked about being labelled as difficult, lazy, a waste of space, not what we wanted, and other variations on the theme of lower down the pecking order.

So is it the child that is being difficult or the very narrow parameters set for them which do not value a day dreamer, a high- energy hyper focused, enthusiastic child who just wants to do stuff? Both these wonderful qualities are quashed, labelled and denigrated by others who are too short sighted and self satisfied to consider that they are causing damage and their perception is mistaken, deeply so.

Yes, I mean actual damage to growing living humans, to children through their formative years, making them doubt their self worth or their options for contributing to society.

Mister or Misses 'Normal', causes damage by prejudgemental attitudes, leaving people undermined, devastated sometimes. It can destroy individual potentials and thus rob everyone of the contribution they might have made to society if normal had not been so myopically prejudiced. We all suffer when one individual does not reach their potential, not in money or status or wealth but in real ways – the creators, the inventors, the out of the box thinkers are often the very people who are not within your narrow band of normal- which ever group of normal you think you belong to. To white people, black is not normal; to black people, white is not normal, to male female is not normal, to 20/20 vision, myopia is not normal.

Who is this normal who evades all prejudice?

Who are you to judge anybody else about anything at all?

We have no idea where our human society is heading – we face more challenges than most people can bear to think about – so they don't, they deny, avoid or counter these truths so they can keep hold of their little bit of whatever they think they have, from the neighbour down the road to the Trump empire. And all of it can crumble in a blink of an eye. In fact it probably will.

Now here is a thought- what if all the diverse groups got together and worked as one to counter this prejudicial attitude, not one group trying to get their voice heard against all the other voices but all work collectively, to achieve a potential positive outcome for everyone. That we all learn to see challenge as opportunity instead of problem! That we all learn to see difference, and value it instead of not wanting to see it! Or if we're forced to see it, fear that it might be hard to manage.   What if we discovered we all really need the hyperfocus of ADHD and the astonishing feats of mental and memory focus some autistic savants have. That these 'gifts' have a huge advantage to humankind elsewhere.

Until we all learn to be open to difference - that this is or is not the right way to do anything, because there are always alternatives to venture into- and the unknown is a challenge but go ahead and try it.

*If we fail to communicate with each other fully, openly, and honestly,
then we cannot connect and we cannot understand.*

We're all collectively responsible for this failure, each of us who makes a prejudgment, an expectation that will be failed, a projection of yourself and what you want from the other, then we never see the other as truly who they are.

Can you not all see how much we all miss out on it then?

We collectively create a climate of prejudice and wonder why we suffer from it. Some suffering a lot more than others, I accept that fully, but nevertheless we all miss out on the wonder - which is diversity - which is variations of themes of what human means – which is every single individual human and for that matter all non-humans too. We can all make steps to drop the prejudices and stop being victims of our own inflexibility and social blindness and start being co-creators of a society where all are valued equally.

Questioning

Jesus outspokenly questioned the received wisdom of the ruling clerics of his day.

Likewise, Siddartha, the Buddha teaches us to question everything, to challenge all that we are told until we are completely satisfied that it is true also for ourselves. Buddha nature is to question our lives constantly, not to be in some state of perfect equilibrium, but to explore, to challenge, and to evolve.

I think I did that throughout life, instinctively really; that was what made life interesting for me, engaged me with staying alive.

I know my parents hated that I questioned everything they ever said - I think that was a huge part of the broken relationship between them and me, and that I could never trust them for anything ever. I never trusted their responses, and they rarely bothered to give me valid explanations. My curiosity for understanding this thing called life was mostly seen as in subordination and rudeness, trouble making and undermining to their authority. To me it was 'well why are we alive then'.

Questioning the accepted world view of your own community can cause trouble for you but it is the best kind of trouble. All the world's great spiritual or divine leaders demonstrate this exact tendency- to question, examine and then challenge. All authoritarian organisations, dictators and country leaders, and statesmen, wish to silence that exact process; they do not want to be challenged or questioned at all.

Currently in the UK the government is disallowing open honest reporting on the real state of the NHS, The Local authorities and the education system. They do this to suppress truths that are simply not acceptable but they think somehow out of sight out of mind they will still get voted in. That is all they care about, not the people whose lives they are ruining.

The opposite of questioning is blind obedience. This is not faith, although many think it is.

Faith comes from a questioned belief not a taught item of faith. I have great faith in my spiritual truths because I have tested them thoroughly in my own life with my questioning, and I have not found them to be wanting, thus I can have wholehearted faith in them. This does not mean that they cannot be modified through further experience. That is an ongoing process, but it does mean that I have some firm ground from which I stand and explore or question further.

Questioning is a process that should never stop.

Questioning can be annoying but it prevents complacency in one's self and does not need to be shared all the time. My husband and soulmate is also my best friend, and we do discuss and challenge ourselves and each other often. It is one dynamic part of our relationship that keeps us both fully engaged every day.

Questions help you to see more clearly, they allow you to look beyond the sacred cows and tightly drawn curtains of illusion. Questions need answers which have some basis of logic or reason in them, otherwise you cannot justify your position.

Just as I challenged my parents, my sons challenged me and it was hard at times- their logic would outweigh my own but it was not to my convenience, or sometimes they could win logically but my experience took precedence.

But I learned from the 'because I say so' school of parenting that this approach for an enquiring mind will not work, will not satisfy, so some kind of explanation might be useful.

Even if that does not fully satisfy, sometimes we all have to learn that we might never know why not, just that why not is the best for now. It is not the questioning that is at fault but the difficulty of the answers that needs our exploration and openness.

So although questioning my parents might have been a contributing factor to their dislike of me, it is also an innate quality that I cannot turn off for anybody. I am just lucky to find someone who also enjoys this approach to life. Similarly if I had not questioned their teaching to me of my worthlessness then I would not have taken this journey and been able to share it with you. I probably would not have made it through at all.

Kinds of questions to ask yourself

Questioning yourself always for your motivation – why did you do that - why are you thinking this – how can you do better - is a good mindfulness practice to check where you're coming from and thus what Karma you might invite back to yourself? If I am unsure how or why I feel a certain way, or why I act in certain ways, I can usually find this by questioning myself closely and then allowing my mind to bring the answer to the surface from the unconscious.

So question everything, leave no stone unturned in your quest to understand yourself and your motivation. This is the basis then for change and growth, becoming more of who you really are and less of the damaged individual who cannot see clearly. Freedom comes from questioning everything, but most of all question yourself, compassionately but firmly – and do not let yourself off the hook.

Relationships

There are literally millions of books and articles that give you the tricks and tips to have a happy relationship but so many of them make fundamental errors in what they say.

The biggest of these is that you must have your own baggage sorted out first before you can have a relationship that will last and be functionally positive.

I disagree.

I disagree from both personal experience and from psychological perspectives too.

I disagree so completely, and I hope to explain why to you.

First of all you are never free of your negatives, they are always there, your baggage is mud, it is your compost. It is good for you too, if uncomfortable at times. Without it you do not bloom so beautifully. Without the mud in life people tend to get a bit carried away with how wonderful they are, they get self satisfied, think they have it sussed, have the answers.

It is only a matter of time until life will show them how that is not what life is about. Life is about humility and that usually means you will need to get humiliated properly until you learn how you are not great. But that is fine. It is self acceptance that matters not self aggrandisement or greatness.

What really matters is not that you get rid of all that emotional baggage first, but that you recognise it is there in the first place, which is a huge part of the humility thing I mentioned earlier. None of us is perfect — we are all works in progress. What society does is to make people feel ashamed of their mud and feel the need to hide it or hide from it.

We need to celebrate the baggage and allow the roses or lotuses to grow better instead of feeling ashamed of it.

We need to stop judging each other generally and especially in relationships. So be open to the fact that you haven't got your issues together yet and that is enough. Be prepared to work on it together. Make it part of your relationship to help each other to face those deep dark inner fears we all have.

What really matters is that you are willing to grow, to learn how to accommodate each other.

The greatest strength in my marriage is that we face each other with gentle kindly love, openness and honesty. My ADHD and post PTSD means I still get triggered sometimes though that is fading with time.

If you take those two things about me, I must be an erratic unstable madwoman to live with. I probably am, but my beloved husband has accommodated these aspects of me because he loves my complexity, my intelligence, my straightforwardness, my sense of humour and sense of fun etc etc.

We also have a great sex life with really deep connections. That is the other thing that really matters. Sex is not a performance but a connection that deepens over time. If it has gone stale, then you probably didn't make that connection when you had the chance. Sex in your sixties is fun, gentle, tender and one of our favourite activities to share. It just keeps getting better. Like our relationship—better by the year in ways that we neither of us would have considered possible, given how much baggage we both had when we got together.

But we have learned trust and communication by working through the baggage together, and that has made us a better couple in terms of friendship, intimacy, compassion, support, being there for each other.

I cannot say how important the sharing really is. Don't get rid of it, that is impossible anyway. Just celebrate the complexity of humanity and learn to appreciate it. My scattiness and tendency to get distracted is just another opportunity for my husband to look after me or support me, although he could get angry with me, but that would spoil our fun lives, so he doesn't. It is all about turning the challenges into fun instead of judgements and anger and expectations being left unmet.

My husband gets more from me than he could ever want in love and friendship and fun though. So the old 'less than perfect' is actually just an opportunity for him to be more loving. And the same thing in return of course. He is far from perfect too (even though I think he is) and I love him for every crazy imperfection he can produce.

Who on earth wants perfect. I don't, that is soo boring. Give me crazy complexity that is honestly expressed and enjoyed too, or comforted if it is hurting of course. It is about being a best friend who does not judge, who embraces and accepts and loves because of the issues.

Please love that muddy baggage in each other, be honest and open about it, work it through together so you grow and learn how to love each other even better. It really is more than worth it.

With that little rant off my chest I shall now look at relationships from other perspectives.

Travelling the Alphabet Emotionally

Relating to others is one of the most important survival skills we need, for emotional, physical and social health and well-being. Relationships are also a source of rich learning, the mirror into which we can look to see our 'self' reflected back as others see us.

Many relationships fell by the wayside during my illness because I just could not cope with other people's stuff since I had more than enough of my own to be dealing with.

Over decades I ended many relationships myself just because I felt I wanted to defend myself before I got rejected any more and I was of course so worthless - so I felt - that no one would want to stick it out with me.

Except those who really got what I was going through and who are genuine people who do not lie or play games with friends. These are still in my life. It's funny that such an illness can clear out all the stuff that you hold on to even though they are not good parts of your life, but when one is well, one can adapt to fit these things - the boiled frog syndrome - because we fear losing people, histories etc.

I have really learned the importance of holding relationships lightly in your hand and valuing them when they are happening in the now, not trying to cling on to mis-matches because of some fear of being alone - this has never been true for me - because being alone is such a rich experience and a sign of mature adulthood (Winnicott). It is also freedom from other people's demands.

I realised that this painful pruning exercise was ultimately a very beneficial one.

A loss of a dysfunctional relationship, where there is a lack of open communication etc is no loss - yet these did tear at my heart strings.

I am such a loving person but I was too hurt to cope with these poor communications and feeling so afraid of them.

So afraid of being misunderstood and judged for the illness, the PTSD, that I became angrily defensive.

I am not proud of that reaction but I also realise I had no choice over it, it was all I could manage at the time. I could not stop myself feeling or behaving like that so I have to embrace all that the PTSD has led me through.

Now I am much happier, fully pruned and less attached to any clingy structures but with a good solid bunch of friends and my sons, and husband, that I could not feel more enriched by their existence in my life. I think this is a large part of the healing process now complete.

The other kind of relationships that ended, that I ended, or avoided until they ended, were those who wanted me to sort it out, to pull myself together, to somehow get fixed on their time schedule. When you are in the middle of a full-on PTSD breakdown it is as much as you can do to stay alive. Being made demands on to please other people just isn't always possible.

The only people who really understood this of me were my wonderful children and my husband who stuck by me day after day after day, allowing me to do what I could manage in a day even if it was just one job in a whole 24 hours.

Sometimes I managed more than that before the exhaustion hit me. Either that or the voices kicked in and I had to go back to distraction activities like watching endless unchallenging 'it's all safe in the end' type dramas on TV.

Now I meet other people with PTSD and I am so sad if they don't have the solid group left after all the pruning, after all the defensiveness and fear has rejected everyone who intends well but just doesn't understand.

It is hard enough to get through with a support team behind you, a dark and terrible journey.

But then I meet others who have made it through to the other side and theirs is an understanding, a shared recognition of the horror of what you have each passed through. The fear of leaving safe spaces, of being with people you do not know to be safe or not, of people who just don't want to know you when you are this fragile or vulnerable.

I am almost back to normal, several years on from the release of that tight grip of fear over me, but the old neural pathways still get triggered from time to time, unintentionally and by people who do know what they are doing, who don't realise they are making judgements about something they know nothing of. This can cut me down still, it doesn't last very long but it can be vicious in its effect on me and my family.

I am able to sense people's energies and nowadays I read them very clearly indeed.

I can tell when someone is genuine or not, even when they don't know it themselves.

I can sense when people make judgements of me or others in proximity I can feel negative energy, self pity and 'dark matter' in people easily enough.

It makes me recoil and I cannot help that, it is just how I am.

PTSD blew me wide open, and I prefer to remain like that for my own reasons, but that openness leaves me slightly vulnerable still, a choice, a preference of mine for sure, just how it is. In return for that sensitivity, I feel so alive, so in touch with all living creatures, so open and flowing in the present moment, and so deeply happy.

It is a price I am happy to pay. So in finale I am grateful to my illness, to PTSD for being what it was, for taking me to places I thought I would never get out of, and for finally showing me what being truly alive means.

Relationships are now far more carefully entered into and cherished, quality rather than quantity.

I can love everybody as fellow humans, but allowing them into my inner circle has to be done very carefully until I know I am beyond triggering any more. I don't judge anybody for being human, just need to be wary of them. We are a very socially complex species.

Responsibility

Who is responsible for what?

You are responsible for your ability to respond, that is what the word means after all, that is what it says.

Can anyone be made legitimately responsible for anything at all?

What is it exactly that we are responsible for?

Basic script is that you are responsible for your thoughts, your words, and your behaviours, in this present moment, and that is all.

But what about an hour ago? Can we really claim that this is no longer our responsibility? Not really. We might say I cannot be responsible for that right now because it is done but we WERE responsible for it an hour ago.

But was that 'us'?

I mean the 'us' that we are now, because that is a different 'us' to the one we were an hour ago too. We have changed, hopefully grown a little, learned from our mistake, regretted the hurt we caused, resolved to be kinder or more careful or more thoughtful next time. We might even have tried to make reparation. So surely we have taken all the responsibility that is possible by now to take from something we cannot undo or not do. If we truly take responsibility, we also heal our self from guilt, shame, and other negative destructive emotions. Once we own our actions and can forgive our self through learning about self compassion, and move on, there is nothing left to do. There is never any going back, just moving on. What we can do right now is to prepare our self for the choices we are about to make, the outcomes of those choices are our responsibility now, but only as far as we can predict them. Realistically though.

We must take responsibility for our choices, since no one else can own them- even if we are coerced into them.

We have allowed that to happen - but we can be gentle with the 'why we allowed that to happen to us', why we are vulnerable to coercion, and learn from that.

Most of all we must be responsible for our journey, our learning, our eternal evolution from one person into another as life does its job of kicking us along one way or another. They are the mistakes we will most certainly make, and learn from, they are ours alone. Uniquely designed to teach us whatever it is we most need to learn next.

Self acceptance, Social Acceptability,

or

Why do we worry about what other people think of us?

Popularity, self-doubt and the gap we fall into between those two. Self acceptance is a huge facilitator for happiness, peacefulness, and a successful life emotionally.

But when we talk of self acceptance, who is this self of whom we speak? Who is it you must accept?

Is it your body, your face, your hair? This is not who you are after all, just the external dressings, the shape, the vehicle through which the real you engages with the art of living. The arms you use to hold another with a loving embrace, the eyes you can see through, the brain that interprets all that input data.

Is it your life context, your job, your qualifications, your status? Are these things fixed? Do we look at a child and judge them according to these measurements? They are just passing aspects of the journey of life but not who you are.

Is it your personality?

What is a personality but a passing thing, an ephemeral expression of how you think and feel in any given moment. You can be wonderful here and less so elsewhere.

I know I am fun to be with when I am relaxed but when I am anxious, I spike out at people. I can't stop it, it's entirely defensive and a reaction based on my PTSD/ traumatised emotional systems. This too will change. So personality is not a fixed thing either, not who you are, but merely a response of yours to the situation you find yourself in at any given moment. Thus I can be all sunny and smiles but also I can be afraid and angry/defensive.

Which is the real me? Both/ neither since I am not fixed but respond conditionally to that situation I find myself in on that particular day/ time /moment. There may be no continuity so how can this be me, or you or anyone else either? And one day I may stop spiking out and thus will my personality have changed or will I just have healed that wounded part of myself?

You are who you are because of everything that has ever happened to you and how you responded or reacted to it, nothing more and nothing less. But this changes on a moment by moment basis, so who you are after reading this will be a different person to the person you were before you read it and so on. We cannot judge others and they cannot judge us with any accuracy at all, with any sense of truth or reality.

Understanding this makes you compassionate to yourself and others and puts an end to all this judgmental unkindness. It silences that inner critic, though you may have to remind yourself of this often. It is also a fundamental and universal truth which is not understood or taught widely enough. The logic is pretty flawless and yet life would be so much better for so many people if we all lived according to this wisdom.

Be the best person you can be in any given moment, the most honest, kindest, open and loving, accepting, forgiving and gentle, and if you cannot manage that in one instance or another then accept that you can work towards this approach and give yourself a break from trying to be perfect. We cannot change those experiences which make us who we are, which brought us to this point, but we can embrace them and accept them and live with them without fearing them.

Then they become our friends and not our enemies and we can be healed with that self acceptance.

Once you can achieve this, you are no longer concerned with the opinions of others, just their wellbeing too.

Just celebrate being the unique person you actually are and accept that this is enough.

Someone somewhere will love you for that quality alone. Self- acceptance is a very attractive quality to have because it makes other people feel relaxed and more confident around you too. Just enjoy the experience of living in your shoes and being you and find out who that might evolve into in time, explore that potential and don't worry about the person who gets left behind each time you evolve, just find out who comes next.

Shame and Guilt

So similar in some ways, and yet so very different, these two emotions can break lives if they get out of control.

The basic difference is that guilt is feeling bad about something you have or have not done, and shame is about you and your general unworthiness because of what you have or have not done.

Guilt first. You can feel generally good about yourself but if you 'let yourself down' in your own terms, then you can make yourself feel pretty guilty. This is far less harmful than feeling utterly worthless because of who you are and everything you do or do not do at any one time.

Guilt can be assuaged by humility and asking for forgiveness or making restitution.

Guilt can do you harm and prevent you from taking responsibility for your choices, actions, and emotions, as can shame.

I have been told and read elsewhere that a little guilt can be good because it acts as a marker, an internal judge or monitor, keeping you on the good path, not letting you fall into bad habits. See if you agree by the end of my argument. I disagree (of course).

Personal development and growth is never benefitted by negative emotions and it is often blocked by guilt and shame. We can become defensive and justify our decisions and choices to show that we were not mistaken. We seek to nullify our guilt and shame by denial, rejection of other points of view and similar tactics, instead of dealing with them at root source.

Often the acceptance of being wrong is one of the hardest things humans are faced with psychologically, and they will fight against it tooth and nail. Guilt or shame are the main reason why.

If they deny their wrongness in this situation, they do not have to feel ashamed or guilty about their action or inaction, so these two emotions prevent them growing and learning from mistakes.

I have fallen into this kind of trap in the past and also had it done to me many times, and it is never a helpful response.

It comes back to being prepared to be wrong which takes humility and honesty, versus being right and defending one's ego sense of honour. Guilt and shame make you less able to stay open and adaptable, unless you are extremely open already, in which case it is not really guilt or shame that has got you, but a realisation that you have made a mistake and have a desire to rectify it.

Let us use an example

Dilemma: A wants to take a holiday for Christmas but there are conflicting demands on their time and resources. There are others who want A and family to go with them and elderly family people who will be left behind and mostly alone.

Choices: –

-takes holiday and enjoys it knowing they can make it up to those others in their own time and that by taking breaks they are taking care of themselves so they are better able and refreshed to take care of others at other times

-doesn't take holiday – and possibly feels slightly or majorly regretful and trapped by person who represents those responsibilities

-takes holiday and ruins it by feeling bad about it so can't enjoy it or get the break they need from the usual routine and possibly even harbours some resentment against person who needs care.

-takes holiday and feels ashamed at their own selfishness but feels guilty about putting themselves first when they have an elderly relative or sick friend to take care of.

-takes holiday or doesn't take holiday but feels ashamed of even thinking they had a right to take holiday.

-rebels against all the guilt and shame, takes holiday defiantly and pretends madly that they are really having a great time, but can't enjoy it because too busy self-punishing. Regrets decision to go and spoils it for everyone else too.

So if you take the holiday without resolving the emotional conflict you only spoil the holiday, even if it is just a slight nagging doubt.

It doesn't matter which choice you make, the point is to make it and take responsibility for it and don't feel guilty about making the right choice for yourself, which ever option is chosen i.e. go and enjoy it or don't go and enjoy it.

We all have to make choices in life and often they are not clear cut. Sometimes it is appropriate to put yourself on the bottom of the needs list and sometimes it is essential that you are at the top of it. Knowing when to do each leads to a pretty guilt and shame free life and these are the reasons for that understanding.

We have to take care of our self, first and foremost, so that we do not become a burden for others when we have burned out, or we start letting people down because we are just too tired to do it all.

If we self -care then we are more able to meet the needs of those less able and less independent than us such as elderly and sick friends and relatives, young children etc.

To heal from an overdose of either you must take responsibility for yourself and your internal processes, thoughts, feelings, belief systems.

All these are ephemeral, no matter how real they feel, and all can be changed if we choose to.

Sometimes shame especially is so ingrained that we feel it is impossible to change that outlook.

But with mindfulness we can begin to see how mistaken and damaged that original emotional position is and was, and we can start to allow ourselves to believe something different.

It is ultimately our own choice but it takes some considerable effort to re-programme our brains to be self-accepting and self-compassionate and to take responsibility for our-selves. It is a process that we have to take in steps, gradually shifting and challenging those thoughts that keep us unhappy and unable to enjoy life to the full.

Now I want to put it from the other perspective. You are the person who is causing the conflict about this holiday. You probably don't know about it since we can all be very good at concealing our true feelings and sometimes that might be appropriate, but would you want to be the cause of such conflict in someone else. It demeans the gift of their time and makes you a nuisance or burden in their life.

I know I would hate that to the tips of my toes. I don't want to be patronised in this way. I want to be valued and if someone spends time with me it is because they like me and want that, not ever out of duty. I would never do anything out of duty but because I choose to and then I have no guilt. I can say 'I will do this and not that,' and everyone knows where they stand.

If you are someone who likes to use duty arguments to get what you want out of people, think how much more delightful it might be to know that instead of extraction you have been given a true gift of someone's love and time. Manipulating through guilt makes you a burden and although you might get what you want superficially, deeper down you have destroyed what you really wanted, what we all want, which is to be loved and valued. You have turned the manifestation of that love into a bribe, a threat, a duty and a punishment.

Once you understand this principle then you know never to do that, to yourself or another person.

When you decide to do everything from choice, and nothing more than that- you are free from the ego's desire to measure your actions, to judge your choices and to decide if you are good or not good. All of that disappears. Instead you can just get on with the job of carrying out your choices. But you will find they are all suddenly much easier and freer, take less energy, and are never a burden or a chore. There is just you, your body and the choice you have made. It is free and easy to do anything when that choice is the place of activity. Only guilt and shame burden you down with resentment or regret for anything.

The other time you may feel guilt or shame is after the event. If you have reason to regret behaving in some way or making a choice that you wish hadn't happened. Again ask yourself if the guilt or shame is going to make that past event any better.

Instead you can let go of the guilt and shame and just make better choices in that present moment of realisation: to forgive yourself, to learn from the event how not to make that same mistake again, to make restitution if possible, and then to move on.

I was on retreat recently and the Nun sister Annabel from the Order of Interbeing talked about emotional hurt and how important it is to rectify it fast. She said if it is left it goes deep and solidifies and is much harder to heal. That is my experience exactly and why I think guilt and shame do not help but we need to have the humility to heal with others quickly, if they will allow it. If not, then that is their choice but there is nothing harder to get over than an unresolved emotional wound.

Ultimately you have to forgive yourself for being less than perfect.

Once you can accept that, then the guilt and shame are also easier to let go of.

Once you are free from this pair of nasties then you can be the best version of yourself because you are no longer twisted into knots and thus you are genuinely generous and happy in your life and gifts to others. Those gifts are honest and openly given, that is their true value.

On a personal note I distrust anything done from duty or social expectation. I distrust it because I wonder what their real motivation might be. What might they be buying from me, negotiating, what am I getting into, will be expected to respond or return with. All of these are the outcomes of duty instead of loving free will. Choosing loving free will works for everyone.

Silence

Words, crashing around,

so much noise, not a sound.

Secret cinema. Private screening.

inner turmoil, silent screaming.

Silence, cracks the din,

opens the heart, lets peace in.

Inner calm, outer glow,

finding truth, start to grow.

Silence and noise are opposites. One cannot exist without the other, one grows from the other. I have loved silence since I learned how to embrace it.

We are taught as children to fill in the gaps with sound, to make our minds ever busy with learning instead of just wonderment at the world around us; for example, at the amazingness of the baby toads that came into our garden every summer and how I would spend my time rescuing them from the lawn before dad cut the edges; at the backdrop of the night sky through my window-gazing time spent when sleep could not come because of the noise in my childhood head; at the peace you find when you climb a tree to the very top and hang in branches only just strong enough to hold your weight, and feel the breeze testing your grip on the rough bark.

The noise was not a soundtrack of my own composition.

It rarely is for any of us. We just replay it until it becomes our own content too.

Travelling the Alphabet Emotionally

As it is for so many of us, it starts with the words of others; adults who filled me with their judgments and anti-wisdom, their hypocrisies and prejudices, their social and superficial values that never gave the child inside a second thought.

They were too filled with their own importance to consider a mere child. Later on, as noise dominated my inner and outer life, I discovered how much it damaged me, so I blocked out the inner noise with music, wallpaper noise, anything to stop the inner noise from drowning my spirit.

Then I discovered Zen and Quakers and retreat and mindfulness and meditation and suddenly silence filled me with joy and freedom. There I found freedom from noise, learned not to take any notice of it most of the time, and everything I had lost as a child returned.

When I step out of the car at night and walk towards the house, I stop and watch the night sky in silence again, perhaps commenting on its glory to my soulmate but still feeling that wonderment which now has room to return. When I walk around the garden, I notice the creatures that live in my garden as it is now, birds, slow worms, an occasional stoat, rabbits (now my old garden).

Silence is the comfort I seek between the busyness of life, the demands of this activity and that commitment. Silence is the gift I give my heart and mind when I sit, alone or in company, and watch my thoughts go by without attaching to them.

Silence is the only bottomless pit as a giver, generous to a fault with her gifts. She gives inner peace, focus, concentration, self-awareness and courage, wisdom and compassion, respite, acceptance, clarity. Indeed she gives everything a heart can long for and a mind can be seeking for.

You cannot 'know' this until you spend time in her company, seek her out at every opportunity. You cannot buy this or acquire it in any acquisitive way.

You cannot achieve this as a goal or try to sneak a grab at it through the backdoor. It comes by open, quiet invitation and constant effort only. You must commit to her gentle embrace, face to face, sit, or stand, or walk with her, invite her into your daily routines, into your heart. It is a life-long commitment, a marriage to your future best friend, your other best friend perhaps.

Silence just is.

TIME

Time is only wasted if you spend it chasing things that are external to you, things out there in the mirage of reality that you think will make you happy or loved, or even just give you temporary relief. Just learning to be with yourself in time makes it timeless.

I need more time

I am running out of time

Time is a measurement that is created by humans and crafted to become a prison of command. It is merely a concept. It does not exist in and of itself. The only time we ever have is the time in this moment.

Have we enjoyed it? Yes, then you have valued your life, your time.

Have you wasted it; how can you waste something that does not exist?

Does something exist if it only a concept?

Time is a concept. Self is a concept. Life is a concept.

Culture, art, war, and everything else, it is all concepts which we have to find a way of negotiating and existing with, loving or hating, fearing or embracing. All concepts capture us with the intensity of their perceived reality, imprison us with the power of the attraction, the convincing nature of their desirability, or repulsiveness.

When it is all broken down to quantum level, it is all just particles.

I spend my time reading many articles about particles so that I can try and understand the true nature of reality more clearly.

We have to navigate these illusions of solidity and reality but we don't have to take them too seriously.

The time we have as consciousness in this form, as human, is limited but the greatest gift we have, until the end. That ending is what makes time appear to be precious, why we cling to its skirts and demand more of it.

We never know when the end might come, sooner or later it will. It is not trite to say that we should value each moment, it is the only way to really live, to be alive until that end arrives, that release from the treadmill of illusions.

How we live matters much more than how much we live.

Is it really that much more sad that some reach that end more quickly or is that the trap that the illusions set for us? How about joyful release?
I love each moment in my life, I look forward to the peacefulness of it ending. Those are not incompatible statements; they represent a truth that we should all embrace. Then we can let go of the suffering and unkindness and fighting and hatred and all the other illusory experiences that make 'this time' so unhappy for so many, the cruelty and ignorant stupidity, so crass and destructively obscene. So unnecessary.
I don't count my time as valuable or lacking value, I don't think anything has a value unless it is the experience of the moment, whatever that is, however that presents itself. We ourselves have the intrinsic power to make it more or less pleasant for ourselves by how many illusions we hold onto in our basket of concepts that make us 'us'; that trap us in the delusion of self and persona and personality. These things exist to us, but not in reality, and thus are not important.
Back to time, can we waste time thinking of abstract concepts like these when these concepts have the power to blast our thinking right out of imprisonment. I think it is time well spent, but that may be my illusion or delusions too, does it matter?

Triggering

I am a sort of expert with triggering—not due to any academic or professional experience and learned academic papers read or researched, but through personal experiences, through experience over many decades—exploring ways to cope with living a normal life, having been traumatised in childhood by both my parents.

There are a lot of people who think triggering is just being upset about something. Having an emotional reaction to something, or someone, which has echoes of one's past about it. Well possibly but that has led to a serious problem with undervaluing the term for describing the experience and downgrading it to 'just people who are too sensitive and sometimes even on the lookout to be upset or offended by something slightly sensitive'.

Let me describe what happens to me when I get triggered.

First of all I feel as if I am instantly frozen in time. Then the back of my head starts to ache with an intensity that is like toothache x 100. This travels down my spine, locking it up rigid. My spine is now quite damaged by these episodes, with long term physical damage, collapsed discs and arthritis due to extensive spasm and tightening of all muscles and tendons until they are damaged. I have had steroid injections and acupuncture needles which have helped massively.

I am emotionally and physically pretty rigid by now and this will have taken just a few moments to take place. Then I am so alerted to any threat, even though my conscious mind knows that none are present. So I am wired and it will probably be several days before I can sleep properly again.

Beta-blockers work in short term for some physical relief and relaxation.

The point is that this happens to my nervous system before I can even think of being upset or not. I am endlessly frustrated by my nervous system doing this to me when it is so patently unnecessary, and I tell it that on a regular basis. Each time I am triggered it makes the feedback loop more sensitive and I am more likely to be re-triggered by lesser stimuli.

I am currently following the research which says, 'stop being triggered so that the nervous system can learn to be less on constant alert'. I meditate often, almost daily, I do yoga, I love to garden, I take long walks, I write and read poetry, I am happily married to the gentlest, most emotionally strong, wise, and even-tempered man I ever met. Equanimity on legs. I am not afraid consciously of any of the things that trigger me. I wish I could be free of it as I feel I could be so much more effective in the world. If I get triggered too much, I start to get symptoms of chronic fatigue back again.

I am not trying to be competitive, the crucial part is that of the automatic response when consciously I am not afraid or even bothered. People are just people, they are a mixed bag and I am happy to take them as they are. I want to stop being triggered more than anything, but for now I just have to live with managing it.

I am not being insensitive to sensitive people but being easily upset is not quite the same thing as being triggered, and it down grades the harsh experiences of some others who are deeply traumatised and 'triggered' in significant ways with long lasting outcomes.

Unfortunately triggering has become a word which engenders as much derision as it does compassion and thus its value is lost for those who really need it to signal a significant problem occurring.

This kind of mild triggering lives in another land called victimhood. A land where people want to identify with groups who have been afflicted and use it as a badge of honour, of belonging. The victimhood approach to life is a form of self-harm and we must be able to self-identify with these differences. It is limiting and closes both you and others around you down. It can often be used as a form of social control, and it ultimately damaging to all. It is often born from an emotional position of judgmentalism and lacks compassion generally. Victimhood is a self-harm because it prevents you healing.

Triggering does not stop you healing from the general experiences of life, but it is a brain **reaction** from the emotional brain regions of the amygdala and hippocampus, which respond before you are consciously aware even that you might be upset by it. This often happens to me, that I think I am fine and then I suddenly find I am locking up and the pain starts, and I hadn't even realised that I didn't 'like' what it was that triggered me. It works on an unconscious level. It sometimes takes me by surprise and is often less about what happened and more about the energy of the people who 'did'. Passive aggressive anger is one of those, I have come to realise.

I am not one of those sensitive to everything types. I am actually quite tough in many ways. I have an attitude to life that includes 'shit happens — get on with it' — including what I went through to get PTSD in the first place — so choose and prefer learning to grow through it instead of 'falling victim to it'. It is a more emotionally healthy attitude but does not in any way underestimate how hard that struggle might be for some, I know it was for me, but I saw how important also. We also all have differing levels of resilience and different emotional neural systems.

Travelling the Alphabet Emotionally

My experience is that you cannot re-frame triggers in terms of content—the amygdala kicks in too fast to rationalise the response and you must just go and calm down and wait for your body to get back to normal.

What we can do though is not attach anything of importance to what happened.

I tend to view being triggered rather like getting a virus, just look after myself until it is gone but don't get attached to the why, it doesn't help.

What I have learned is that I don't get triggered for no reason- the energy must be significantly wrong in some way or another, and beta-blockers do help me to get right back down as fast as possible, so I now carry them with me.

My reframe is that these triggered episodes are helpful to me, letting me know that it is not ok—the world is not filled with peace and harmony, and that is just how it is. It is also not my responsibility to sort it all out and all I have to do is just breathe through this next moment until it all settles down again.

It has all left me broken open nowadays and I do have to live carefully, but that openness is also a fantastic gift which brings with its insights into all sorts of things.

There is other research which says to keep practising deep mindfulness which I have been doing for 25+ yrs. now—the overdeveloped stress response systems gradually become less reactive, they shrink, and the happy ones grow- so the severity of triggers reduces slightly.

But for instance, I was in the middle of a stress response/ triggered period because I was going somewhere at the weekend, which I wanted to go to, but my brain knows that there are risks associated from the past. I tell it 'not likely to occur' but my unconscious goes 'nevertheless possible'. So I was not able to sleep properly and was slightly wired even though I badly wanted to go to this place and my husband is even coming with me for the first day just to help me stabilise but then has to leave me there—amongst friends too—but I am still being triggered badly and it is extremely frustrating, life limiting and exhausting. My meditation practise has given me huge transformation over the years but is still unable to overcome the triggering in my body—YET! I did make it, needed medication to get through the first 24 hours and then coped for the second day, but the return home toll on me was complete exhaustion for several days.

I live in hope for myself that this sensitivity I have to live with will ease in time and that I learn all the lessons it wants to teach me, but I do find that the less often I am triggered the less severe the reactions seem to be, although a neighbour who shouted at me is now someone I am soooo wary of I can't stop myself watching him in a 'starey wary' sort of way, as in defensive, 'prey style towards predator' because that is what it feels like. Perhaps I am being shown compassion for prey animals?

I don't hide behind my triggering, but I cannot always stop it or adapt my behaviour accordingly and I have only been working with this for 60 years— this is as far as I have got with managing the situation. My preference—to live away from all people except those I know who are safe—it may be possible one day soon.

Being triggered is now recognised properly by most professionals and other people except those who do not allow humans to be honest and vulnerable, and whilst I agree it can be overused, it is generally identifiable from any other response and certainly not remotely the same as being upset. By comparison that is a doddle to get over and takes no time at all.

As a very mature adult in both years, life experience and attitude to life I can assure you that I am fully emotionally responsible for myself. I just cannot stop it, but I can and have learned how to deal with it, including not to blame the person who triggers me, I know they do not mean to. But this does not mean it doesn't happen, it is a deep automatic amygdala-based response with which I am working very hard to gain some management input but that takes a lot of effort and time and is very iterative. Thus I am almost grateful nowadays for my triggered moments, as they show me I am succeeding—I am slowly reducing their strength and impact BUT I AM NOT JUST UPSET, THERE IS A HUGE DIFFERENCE BETWEEN THE TWO.

I can do this. I will do this!

Fortunately, I am amazingly happily married, and my husband totally gets me so if I say I need out of any situation, he helps me achieve that too, without that I most certainly would still be a legally drugged-up junkie in hospital or else dead. He is my safe space, wherever he is I can fold against him and feel safe and he will hold me until I am stable again. So, thanks to him and a few understanding friends, I can have a rich and full life. I am grateful to my triggers as they give me something to keep working on for my mindfulness practice and each time I am triggered I do not give it power other than to make myself feel safe enough to get on top of the process. It is a process that my amygdala body goes through and I cannot stop it, but I am slowly dismantling it, as I have been doing for my whole life time, 63 yrs., but now I have really good tools to do it with that actually work and are slowly rolling back the severity of triggers.

Travelling the Alphabet Emotionally

I agree that standing up to your triggers is one way to go but it is a very hard and brave way to go and might be counterproductive, Nevertheless I have recently identified one triggering source that I will stand up to next time it is appropriate. Someone can only make this decision for them self though if they feel prepared to take this risk for them self.

If I was forced to fake it through my PTSD as I was so often in childhood, I think I would completely collapse again, even now. Often you do not know when something will trigger you , but you can take responsibility for it once you have faced it and it has happened.

Please be gentle with people who get triggered—it is a kind of living hell, and don't use the word lightly—it leaves us with nothing.

Trust

Trust is a magically powerful emotion to have.

It can utterly transform a life, or breaking trust can utterly destroy it too.

Trust can be fragile, easily broken, difficult to establish in a solid way. Trust is possibly the most underrated dimension in close relationships of all kinds, lovers, family connections etc.

Trust starts with yourself. But it is learned through your parents. They should be your first model of trusting in relationships, in other people.

I learned that home was the most unsafe place to be and parents could most certainly never be trusted. Not their love, not their physical touch, not their words or their deeds either. I just learned that I had to rely on myself only, and never to trust others, especially family.

But I had also been made to feel utterly unlovable. So I always trusted on a 'testing out' basis, the 'waiting for the betrayal'. In this I know I am not alone. How many people can you truly trust?

I went through life not even really trusting myself since I crashed every so often. No matter how much effort I put into my life and I really worked hard to make it a good life, I always felt that it would fail on me. That was a judgement placed upon me which I mistakenly embraced too.

In that wonderful way of self-fulfilling prophecies of course that older judgement worked, and I would collapse both emotionally and outwardly too. But I was fiercely defensive and determined not to show it.

And then I would get up and dust myself off, and full of shame and a sense of failure I would start to build my life once more. It never occurred to me that I could trust in myself that I could always start again. I only measured the failures. Back then I did not see how much I was growing each time, how much I was learning and becoming wiser at this human living game. It took me years to discover that one.

In relationship terms also, my parent's influence on my early ability to generate trust in others meant I was always just waiting and eventually of course something would happen that would prove me right. It did not occur that I would also let people down or make mistakes. It was always me watching externally, not internally, watching everyone suspiciously, but also in desperation to be loved or valued.

The point came when I would begin to turn this all around. First of all I had to learn to trust myself and this came in stages, learning how to maintain my own sense of values and integrity.

I found my spiritual journey in the most concrete form it had ever manifested itself to me before hand, and it probably would be fair to call it my obsession for the first few years. I jumped from this theory to that one, searching for something concrete to fix onto and place all my trust into. I was on a mission and ended up learning a lot of key lessons.

First, I had to learn to trust myself and my own intuition. I had ignored it so many times and that was always part of my downfall. I explored that in depth and it led to my second book too.

I found I was more intuitive and deeply sensitive to the energies of the world than I had ever allowed myself to believe before. I re-tuned into that and learned how to understand it. It led to me deciding to write, wanting to learn how to write, and then admitting to myself that I am a writer, that is now what I mostly do.

Despite so many people really letting me know they thought very little of my writing skills, that my aspirations were ridiculous, I got a contract.

It was out of the blue and an astonishing piece of synchronicity. But I was still very distrustful and was not the easiest person for my publishers to work with. I did four books with them though over four years. My trust and distrust in other was still undermining my life so profoundly. I was still struggling with myself but that is not such a bad place to write books from.

A few more similar events led me to look more deeply into trust once more. By then I had also met the love of my life and after twenty-one years together we are still as much in love as ever. But this relationship brought out all my trust issues deeply. We both made mistakes in our early years and were also faced with a huge number of complications and challenges which should have brought us down. But it didn't.

We had such a strong bond. Once I accidentally wrote happily welded bliss instead of wedded bliss, and then laughed because it seemed that was how we were with each other. Welded. No matter what life threw at us it seemed that we would always find something that kept us together. Nothing broke us up. We felt invincible and yet I still felt insecure inside, still testing the water. Just in case.

But all the while my soul-mate never let me down. By then we had shared everything possible from our histories, I had gone through a complete breakdown, I had gone through so many crazy spiritual experiences, and still he was always there, always fun to be with, always kind, gentle and loving. I was finally able to trust physically, emotionally, socially. On every level I realized that I could trust our love for each other, that we were fallible human beings, that we could both make mistakes, but our love would always see us through.

I learned to relax completely into physical touch, to trust the way his hands held me, with tenderness that would not suddenly turn into violence. To trust his eyes, his integrity, his steadfastness, his honesty. To trust our lovemaking, our deep, deep emotional and spiritual connection. It was all healing through the layers.

Then I went on a retreat about grounding oneself in spirit, and in places. But I realized that neither was my grounding. Love was my grounding. Not just ours though.

By now I'd had so many profound spiritual experiences, which I've written about in depth elsewhere, and deeply realized that there is groundlessness in the nature of existence, that to anchor myself to something material was a pointless thing.

I learned that trust has to be based on the inner wisdoms of the spirit and that love is the key to it all. In deep meditations I have experienced a profound sense of love for all living beings regardless of their external appearances or their behaviours. I may find them more specifically challenging but although I was, and still can be very distressed by the externals, the internals are still based on love for all at all times.

Coming on a journey of such deep distrust of self and others, I can tell the difference between living with and without trust. Without trust things so often fall apart because you are ungrounded and unstable inside. The outside always mirrors the inner life, the brokenness of a life without trust showed through.

The difference is extraordinary.

Learning how to relate to your-self in a trusting manner is a healing process in the extreme. Learning that you can manage the twists and turns of life and falling down doesn't matter.

Learning that life is not a smooth ride, but you will make it through if you can just trust that process of surrendering to the lessons it gives you along the way.

Learning to trust your own intuitive senses, to trust your deeper wisdom.

Learning to trust physical contact as something beautiful and magical with those you love. Learning to trust that when it doesn't feel ok then it probably really is not ok at all.

Learning to trust the process of your life, the journey, the stages and transformations along the way, the realizations, the wisdoms.

Learning to trust my husband's embrace, that it can soothe and calm me when I am distressed instead of making me feel trapped and dominated.

Learning to use casual touch all the time as a way of making contact with people, to let them know you 'see' them and are not just going through the motions, that when someone is low then a gentle slight touch can help them feel that connection of human love to human soul and perhaps a little release of oxytocin that helps someone to feel better.

We often say all we need is love, but although I agree, alongside that you also and equally need trust. It should never be taken for granted. When you have broken someone's trust, you might just have broken their life, so think carefully before you risk that. Trust yourself enough to know your own motivations and trust them.

Uncertainty, unhappiness, all the Uns.

What is an 'un' but an absence of the thing it is 'un' to. Unkindness, unhappiness, uncertainty, unbelievable….. the list goes on.

I want to look at this concept of un specifically rather than any one version of un.

So this is an absence of something we think 'should be there' or 'should be different' to how it is. Yet it isn't and thus we are mourning its lack of presence.

Of course we all prefer the positive. It makes our lives easier and more comfortable and we are less challenged to find the depths of both our strengths and our weaknesses.

And that is the point. We need the 'uns' as much as we need the lack of 'uns' in life, but everything in balance. How can we perceive the value of light if we never have darkness and the relief of sleeping in darkness if we only have light, and so on, with everything?

The opposites only exist in relationship to their counter-part, without one you cannot have the other.

So unpleasant gives us pleasant, unkind gives us kind. This is the dualistic way of perceiving, thinking and living which we humans have embraced for centuries. It is not how life really is though.

Scientifically speaking there is no duality, there is just oneness. One planet, one substance called water, one atmosphere etc, AND we are all a part of that. We cannot survive apart from that, we are not self sufficient without air, water, earth, other people, plants, animals, to keep us alive. We are all interdependent and thus need everything to be at its best to give each of us its best.

If we only see in 'un' terms we are victims, disempowered, helpless... but we also become destructive in our attempts to protect ourselves from them.

And that destructiveness is self destructiveness because if one part goes rotten then it can spread to the rest very quickly.

And what are we protecting our self from in reality?

Nothing that exists except in our perception!

Nothing that can hurt us unless we refuse to recognise its value to us and allow the fear of that particular un to engulf us in self-pity!

Embracing the unkindness and unhappiness does not mean pretending it is fine. Accepting it just means accepting it also exists and if we resist it too much then we resist the benefits of the balanced approach to life. Once we embrace it in ourselves and in others we can then start to do less of it to each other. That surely is the ultimate goal in life. I am glad of plenty of 'uns' in life – I learn far more from them that I do the easy stuff, but balance is ideal.

Victimhood.

This is a position we take in our life and it is a choice. I don't have a lot to say about this because much of it is said elsewhere in this book.

The alternative to victimhood is empowerment.

Victimhood is a passive and unengaged mental and emotional attitude or position towards life and its events, and often leads to other conditions such as narcissism, depression, failed relationships and other sorts of life problems. It is of itself already egocentric and thus heading towards narcissism.

Own your mistakes, work to heal your-self and take responsibility for your own life. That is empowerment.

The only true victims are those whose freedom to choose is taken away from them. Young children who are abused are victims because they are too young to have self agency. Slaves and captives are victims for similar reasons.

The rest of us are not, so really have no excuses.

We are in the middle of our own life, each of us, and we each have to balance the things we can control over the things we cannot control. Not being able to control other things does not make you a victim of them, you can still choose how to respond to them, that is your responsibility – your ability to respond. Sometimes things influence us but we still have to take responsibility for being influenced in a certain way and then change that. Just don't be a victim but learn to balance what you can take responsibility for against what you cannot, and then act accordingly. 'I did that stuff because this stuff happened to me', but was that your only choice? Maybe the only one you understood at the time – so learn a better way, explore and be adventurous in your life.

Mess-up big time, that is OK if you then learn and grow and move on from it.

But if you wallow in victimhood at the conditions that made you mess up, you will never heal. MY ADHD makes me mess up often, nowadays I don't put myself into positions that mean I will probably mess up and more, but I also work tirelessly to not mess up and to master my ADHD tendencies that can be dysfunctional.

When you overcome your need to be a victim you will have better relationships, better mental health, and a better life free from many of the negatives like guilt, shame, lack of trust. Once you stop being a victim you start to trust yourself and feel less at the hands and whims of others.

I cannot emphasise enough how important this lesson was to me and how much I can see that others suffer needlessly for not addressing it in themselves.

V is for Violence

I abhor violence. I am capable of violence. One thing I am not is nonchalant about it.

It is not a commonplace experience for me anymore, as it still is to some people, and this matters deeply to me.

Violence is never a good thing though it may be understandable in certain circumstances. I have made commitments to live my life without violence and denying war, as part of my commitment to Quaker principles and thus my membership of my local meeting.

There are only four commitments we have to meet for this membership to be honoured, to uphold equality for all, to be on a clear spiritual journey, to be committed to environmental protection and climate change reversal and to commit to the Quaker peace pledge against all forms of violence and warfare.

I have also made similar commitments to my Buddhist Zen Master through the 5 Mindfulness Trainings, and my study and commitment, yet to be made formal through ordination, of the fourteen Mindfulness trainings which include honouring life and preventing violence as profoundly as possibly whenever it may arise.

My strongest direct experience of violence was also one of my earliest experiences in life, starting at around 3-4 years of age. This was when my mother turned on me. Her violence was limited to extreme physical shaking and shouting at me at that age – turning red in the face with rage and foaming at the mouth in her hatred of me because I was not the daughter she wanted and she was pregnant with the child that was to be my sister who would take my place and be what she wanted after all. I was now surplus to requirements and an anathema to her from that point onwards.

Violence then grew from my father who was told repeatedly that I was causing my mother to be so unhappy and if only he would punish me enough to make me bend to her will, she would be happy again. Since then I have lived with Post Traumatic Stress Disorder, although now mostly healed apart from triggering, which I am now working on energetically! Violence in childhood begets more violence. It teaches you that your body has no worth because it can be attacked, and sometimes even damaged, by those who are supposedly your carers.

Domestic violence is wrong on every level.

It comes to something when at 15yrs, just after your parents have split up, your dad apologises for having hit you so hard previously but justifies it with 'I wanted to hit your mother but I hit you instead because I knew I could stop myself killing you'.

That was supposed to make me feel better?

Just let those words sink in for a few minutes.

This is what happens when violence is the only way of coping with strong emotions in a dysfunctional family. People use each other as scapegoats to express and project their emotions onto because they have no other option available to them that they know how to use. Their emotional literacy is so low that they have no options available to them than violence. I have written elsewhere about exactly how my parents came to this place together, but their/ my story is not so uncommon.

There are many kinds of violence available to families to mete out onto each other. The obvious physical and or sexual violence of course come to mind immediately, but this is not necessarily the worst part of it.

Travelling the Alphabet Emotionally

Emotional and spiritual violence is equally damaging, if not more so, since it is invisible and insidious. It comes in various forms that all seek to make the individual feel utterly worthless and can leave lasting damage to children's developing nervous systems. It creates unbalanced stress / happiness systems where the stress, on guard alertness system, is over developed and the happiness chilled out systems are severely pruned back. Whilst this can be reversed or ameliorated, it takes decades to undo this damage, done so easily and thoughtlessly at the optimum time for neural development.

The alternatives of listening and compassion are so obvious but only available to you if you understand them, have experience of them, or have learned to use them.

Most violence stems from fear in its many forms, with anger as the front man to feel strong in the face of your own fear. I realise now that both my parents were afraid of each other but were unable to express that or come to any kind of reconciliation. I have little recall of them ever being nice to each other though. They had been married for about three years before I came along. I think I was supposed to heal all the cracks that had appeared between them by then and of course all a child does is to expose them even more.

I came from an era when hitting children was normal and there was no obvious sense of it being wrong as far as my parents were concerned, at the time. Although clearly my Dad did realise it was not ok at deeper levels. What had happened I think played on his mind for the rest of his life so cutting me off was the only way he knew how to manage that too.

The trouble is that when hitting and anger are combined, they are a deadly weapon.

Anger is actually always against the self but the self wants to abdicate responsibility and project it out onto other people in 'self-defense'. Thus the 'you made me do it' or 'she/ he must have provoked him/ her' attitude.

It is all far more common that we would want to acknowledge and is a result of the fundamental lack of deep understanding of human psychology, both male and female.

Trying to force people to see that they are 'wrong' mostly makes them more entrenched in their opinion in the first place. That this is mistaken is obvious, that we need to educate people to see more clearly and to know what is their responsibility, and what is not, is also essential. It takes guts to speak out against one's 'clan' on issues like this and you can risk getting alienated yourself.

This happened to me with much of my own family, and then gradually certain members of the family came back to me and listened more deeply, and actually saw the sense in what I said. Some just thought of me as difficult because I would not follow their position and 'fit in'. I didn't mind that because to me speaking out against injustice is more important. Anyone who does not take a really strong stand is in a way still colluding; anyone who is unwilling to risk their own 'comfort' for the sake of someone who is suffering is still colluding.

Writing about it for me has been a crucial step of my own fight back and for the greater good, learning how to heal, how to escape the cycles of self abuse which ensued, to go public, to stand up to, and risking the outcomes of that, sticking your neck out so that the perpetrators see they are not condoned. They are damaged people but their actions create a great deal more damage, the cycle we need to talk about and bring to an end.

That is a whole paradigm shift for the whole of society. That will take time and education and compassion, it is not easy to look at yourself and find you are wanting, less than perfect yourself, colluding.

This is why it needs to happen from childhood up.

- If we educate generations of children into compassionate ways of viewing the world and all who live on her,

- If we teach children how to self soothe and cope in challenging situations.

- If we teach them how to stand their ground and know their own truth,

THEN we empower a whole generation to say no to all forms of violence.

And once we stop domestic violence, we probably stop community violence, ecosystem violence, racial violence, in fact all fear-based violence can be reduced down to a minimum once we stop being afraid of each other and learn to be loving and compassionate instead. We don't need to like everybody, just have compassion for their humanity and differences or similarities to ourselves.

Once we also learn to view ourselves compassionately, people can be encouraged that life is better if you take this approach, and although it can be challenging, it is far happier for you too, because you are at peace inside with your own self/ soul/ whatever you want to call it.

This is possible as has been shown in a few cases where fear has been actively worked, such as through law enforcement models in Florida which I read about recently. Just think how much more powerful that would become if we taught a whole generation of children this approach to life.

Worrying

Worrying is one of those pointless activities that our brains engage with, and more or less we all do it.

This is a short chapter because it is really quite a simple issue to challenge. So let us break it down.

We usually worry about something that might happen in the future, it can only be something that 'might happen' – even if it is based on previous experience, we cannot know for sure it will happen like that.

Ask yourself these questions –

- did worrying about it stop it in any way
- did it make you feel better?
- did it help other people?
- did it make you more effective at helping sort it out afterwards?
- did it change the future at all?

Worrying is completely useless and what is more it is selfish and a burden to others who then feel obliged to act to stop you worrying. We hold each other back endlessly through worrying. One of the most common reasons people give for not attempting to do something spectacular in their life is that they didn't want to worry someone else.

Stop worrying and be open to what the future holds for self and others. Learn from the past and change patterns of choices that leave you feeling regretful. Don't hold yourself back or use worrying as an excuse not to do something. Do it or don't do it but own that decision. Own your life, and accept it will have challenges to face, but understand that worry will only undermine you and those around you.

If I had not done the things that I did to stop others worrying, my life would be so awful now that I cannot describe.

It is not narcissistic to live your life and own it, as long as you take responsibility for it, consider other people as far as you are able to and make choices that fit with your own internal value system and which will not actively harm others.

Wrongness, being wrong and being right.

This is a huge topic for me, as huge as the ocean, and one so close to my heart; thus I want to go deeply into it.

My mother had to be 'right'. It was part of her NPD (narcissistic personality disorder) and almost a religion for her. Her NPD also made her a bare faced liar and an astonishing purveyor of double standards.

As a child, with her as a 'role model', I simply survived her worst and learned some very confusing messages about life. I also learned some bad habits and had to unlearn them the hard way. I was not able to self delude as remarkably well as she did and when I fell foul of my own mistakes in areas of honesty and rightness, it felt terrible inside.

She could never be wrong because she could not bear that 'one admission' which would expose the huge vast ocean of wrongness's she had committed in her long and unhappy life.

That may be a clue to why many of us have similar problems in accepting we are wrong. But lying about it or blank denial doesn't help if you want to have genuine and wholesome relationships with others. You must learn to come clean, be humble, and allow yourself to be mistaken when necessary, and to allow others the same fall from grace without making it feel worse for them. Making them feel safe to be fallible is the most loving gift you can give anyone. It is liberating on so many levels. It allows you to be genuine.

I come from a wider family where jeering at, and ridiculing someone for being mistaken was seen as an acceptable sport. I once sat at a family members meal table and saw them take their son apart. He said something incorrect, but unimportant. They all jumped. I saw the fleeting pain in his face before he put on his armour and laughed too. They did not notice what they had done, but I did, and I have never sat at that family meal table since. It left a deeply shocking memory for me, which my young relative probably won't even recognise since he was so swift to conceal his true hurt. I learned yet again that pats of my family were not a safe place to be.

Being 'right', as in believing you have the moral upper-hand, or that your opinion should be inviolable, is a not uncommon position for us all to take in certain sets of circumstances. We believe we know something absolutely to be right. We know our right from our wrong. We have our resolute core values to which we adhere endlessly, vigorously, and to the depth of our being.

But we really need to re-think some of that, for several reasons.

Our knowledge or perception may be seriously flawed for starters. But our need to be right means we will be unable to recognise our wrongness because we are blinkered by our own paradigms.

Then there is the arrogance of the personal perceptual position, without an in-depth awareness of one's own conditioning, social, familial and experiential, including our rebellion against those influences, if we have taken that approach to life, as I have. Thus I / we have an individual paradigm of the world, of experiences, of life that is entirely subjective and thus immediately flawed. It is also species-centric most of the time too, another whole layer of error potential.

Nevertheless, there are universal truths, the kind of undeniable realities which can feel like an inconvenience to us and are thus diverted from consciousness. Obvious ones for me are climate change, interconnectedness versus individual gratification, whether money has any real value to us as humans, and such like. Cycles of life and death, birth and decay also fall into this irrefutable truth bracket, of constant change, impermanence, etc. And yet we so rarely consider these truths when thinking deeply or even just passing reflections about things, life, the universe etc.

These truths for me override anything personal. These are undeniably 'right'.

These universal truths are still basically human species-centric but nevertheless effect the entire planet and all who live on her, including us. When we construct truths, which do not take these universal truths into full account then we are more than likely deeply mistaken in our position. We ignore them at our own peril.

Being right can lead to all sorts of problems for you and society as a whole. I am not advocating the opposite position of people-pleasing and social conformity at the expense of standing up for moral values and ethical principles. In fact, I advocate the opposite. That is a weakened position which has led to many of the worst evils in the world. Just by not getting involved even, we can give passive permission for serious crimes against humanity or the natural world. It is called wilful blindness. By stating 'that is politics' and 'I don't do politics', we are colluding with numerous atrocities meted out against countless individuals of whatever species you care to mention.

That everything is political is something of a given for me, but for many people this is not the case. Everything has political implications. Health care, education, housing, taxation and employment, social security systems, food, the countryside, reproduction rights, freedom of speech, crime and punishment, state theft.

I could go on, but all this affects everybody every day one way or another and therefore it is all political.

Unfortunately, politics becomes mired in ideology and self interest and is thus open to many abuses, according to the moral compass of those who get into political power. But behind them are, often, un-elected power brokers who are far more sinister. They use money to buy influence to gain more money and power and to be able to trash even more people's lives. I am not joking here, nor am I scare-mongering. I also know that history shows us that great wrongs are more or less always righted in the end. Life has a habit of going in circles too large for us to understand in our own short lives but large enough to explore when looking back at history creatively and openly. Yet politics is one area where being right or wrong has become a source of the most astonishing levels of dishonesty believable, self interest being the main motivation, which overlooks the whole higher truth of interdependence and inter-connectedness.

In order to understand why 'being right' seems so important, we need to look at what being wrong represents.

The first important point is that it always comes from a place of insecurity, specifically insecurity of the EGO, our sense of self, our self esteem, and our self image. Being 'right' defends that ego as if it is a real thing.

Ego is not real of course, but mostly we are fooled into thinking it is real because to us it feels real. It is our self image, identity, self worth, status, goals and achievements in life. The higher you climb on the back of an Ego, the harder the fall, the more violently you will fight to protect it. All a huge misunderstanding. The ego is simply what you think you are, or who you think you are, before you drop away from that belief system and start to see yourself more clearly.

The person you consider yourself to be is an historic collation of ideas and memories. These are only the basis of who you are now, but they are not who you are beyond the moment they occurred in, right back then. You have changed multiple times since those moments and thus are no longer the same person. There may be some sense of continuity of course but essentially you are someone new.

If you need to be right based on who you are, you are stifling the growth and emergence of the future you in all their wonderful potentials.

We are reborn every minute, in that we are a new potential waiting to be discovered, and mostly we only see the old self and adhere to those routines and patterns of behaviours, choices and ways of being in the world. We limit our access to deep wisdom by admitting only ideas that confirm we were already right and thus have nothing more to learn from life or experiences. We 'know' it all already. We are right, so why should we bother with being open to ideas that make us question our adopted position of 'rightness'.

And here you can rightly challenge me as to if I think I am right or not in this book thus far. Well yes, I think I have something valuable and important to say but I am open to further challenges to my belief system. Actually, I thrive on them. I cannot imagine living and not having my eyes opened on a regular basis to new thoughts and impressions and paradigms. But yes I think there is some truth in what I am writing about here. It is where I am today, who knows next week?

What I have learned about being right myself though is how I express my views. There is little point in haranguing people with my ideas. That will not enable them to make quantum leaps in their own depth of understanding or be able to embrace my ideas into their own and thus stretch us both further.

Many of my ideas I throw out in shorter thought pieces and publish online, which others will dismiss as being insubstantial. They may only express a single perceptual stance.

Possibly, but only for those already converted to a more open way of exploring life on planet earth in the 21st century, or those who only want factual arguments based on stats which support the argument. I can do that, but this section of the book is not about that, it is about my experiences, a solipsism approach to understanding the Dharma, healing from abuse and emotional intelligence.

But a small piece about something relatively inconsequential may just open a chink of insight, a slight cracking in their armour of being 'right already and having nothing more to learn'. These short pieces sow seeds lightly, so there is room for them to germinate. That is my intention. Then they may take some time to develop and grow and come upon another similar notion and the two of them may link up. Then someone may go through an 'AHA' experience, as I have done many times, when everything I thought I knew was tossed aside and I was faced with a whole new world of reality, which was scary as hell but has proven to be a fantastically varied and insightful journey through life.

If we are already too 'right' to allow ourselves to be taken on such journeys we are sorely lacking the meaning of life and are living an existence of mediocrity and emptiness.

This is where the marketing people step in.

'YOUR LIFE IS BORING AND HUMDRUM, LET US ENTERTAIN YOU WITH THIS LATEST THIMGUMY THAT YOU CANNOT LIVE WITHOUT.'

Except you can of course, but now you need this thingumy to fill the gap in your 'rightness' that has left you empty and separated from the joy of being alive and living in each moment.

I have repeated the following quote often, reportedly from the Dalai Lama and other such figures of wisdom.

Do I want to be right or do I want to be happy?

It is such a great question. If it is an either/or, as I have found it to be, then of course I choose happiness. I don't mean the transient fleeting happiness of having stuff, material wealth and trinkets. I mean deep down to the 'tips of your toes' happiness. I mean being deeply in love with your life on a daily basis and only occasionally being knocked off course by the sudden demise of someone, or shocked by the speed in which life can change on you. Or in my case being triggered back into PTSD!

But the deep happiness doesn't depart in these moments, it is just temporarily subsumed perhaps, waiting for the dung-heap to settle before it can re- emerge even brighter and stronger than before. No mud no Lotus, always.

Being right blocks humility and thus separates you from others, all others, even those who agree with your brand of rightness. This is because it is a 'rightness' sense of belonging based on fear of not belonging. We only make really true and deep connection with others through our vulnerability, not through our strength or rightness. By valuing 'rightness' over 'connectedness' and acceptance we exclude people, enforce them to conceal their tenderness and hide it from us, just as my nephew did at the family meal table. Instead of being embraced for his vulnerability, he was obliged to conceal it as a survival choice.

I had to do that so many times in my life whilst still involved with family that I no longer mix with them. The traces of mother are embedded through-out, she was after all also a victim of that family system in many ways and simply embodied it at its worst. I have no interest in dealing with that energy any more. The family were too 'right' for me and did not want to hear my voice on anything. There are better choices to be made.

I have a wonderful family of my own, a deeply humble and open loving relationship with my husband and sons, and a wealth of friends and companions of all sorts whom I value greatly. Some share my world view, and some do not but we do not need to argue about it or silence each other either and that is the point. Openness to conflicting points of view is paramount. We may have a point but so may they also.

There cannot be a right or a wrong, just a journey of discovery to the heart of what life means, but there can be a right or wrong attitude to being right. And that attitude can do a lot of harm on the huge world politics stage or in a small family way. It is all the same problem.

If you are 'right' have you considered you may be mistaken—my favourite Quaker advice and query and one to which I return often. I am still on my journey to the heart of what it means to be alive and human, but I have found deep joy, open tender love, resilience to life and astonishment at the amazing journey which is life. Being open to new learning is not being wrong, it is just admitting you have not already got all the answers, so if you want a right, then choose that approach, it can't do you any harm. The alternative can though.

Xtras to Zany

A chapter for the madness, which helps life to be fun and happy and joyful. Life is just fun, except when it isn't. It can also be extra-ordinary. But we often overlook the potential for fun – for madness – for being crazy or zany or whatever word you want to call it, in the name of being sensible. We so often lose the joyfulness of childhood when we lose the childishness that went with it, we risk losing that at our own cost.

I'm unable to avoid the odd dark times occasionally but as I have said else where they just make the good times that much more enjoyable. And I do celebrate all those good times with joyfulness and my own brand of madness.

ADHD has been the joy and bane of my life and has earned me a bit of a reputation for being unpredictable, possibly a little zany.

A young girl I once knew nicknamed me Mrs. E. It was apt. When I am on a high I get very 'jump up and down, run around fun mad zany'. This is no Bi-polar mad – I have lived with that and it is not the same. Instead it is sheer exuberance and I can manage it, but why would you want to. Why would you not want to enjoy the best part of having ADHD?

If I am happy, I can just stand and jump up and down with my hands on my husband's shoulders for ages and he just waits for me to stop and gives me a hug- he knows I am in a good mood and excited about something and that is joyful for him too. It balances his very constant equanimity. It is a good mix. Sometimes he joins in and jumps with me too and that is shared joy in abundance.

By nature though I am fairly introvert and I like to be alone and with silence. This was true of me as a child until so many people made me feel there was something wrong with me for being like that. People saw the energy of the ADHD hype and thought that was the real me.

But mostly I wanted to curl into chair and lose myself into a book or be out in the countryside. Mostly I like to be quiet.

One of my most vivid memories was with an old school friend whose house backed onto fields and countryside. One weekend we went exploring the fields, collecting dried flowers along the way for her mother. I didn't want to end that walk. I still feel like that now when I am out in the countryside around my home, but my legs and joints cannot walk like a fifteen-year-old anymore.

Another dimension of zany is also probably part of my ADHD / ASD brain, that I see genitals everywhere. I had never noticed this thing in life until my uncle pointed out that several wallpaper designs by William Morris were depiction of female genitalia.

I had never seen female genitalia at that point so was fascinated- it was before the advice given to young women to explore their own nether regions and become familiar with them.

A while later on, the same 'walking in the countryside friend' had a slightly eccentric father who liked to lunge at us young teens with a knife and then ask why we flinched, saying we were supposed to see the knife as a phallus and go towards it. From then on I began to notice phallus and vulva shapes in everything. I wish I couldn't see them sometimes but I just do, in abstract or just by accident.

It does make my husband laugh out loud, for which I'm grateful. What can be more fun that to make your beloved laugh from shock after over two decades of close togetherness.

Nowadays I would suggest that both these men were out of order to talk or behave like that around fifteen or sixteen-year-old girls.

But back then sexism and male dominance / sexual bullying was so common place you didn't even notice it. I do remember feeling shocked both times though and, more significantly, quite uncomfortable.

But I am left with that legacy. I cannot 'not see them'. So I just play with that tendency and have fun with it instead. I have learned when not to express it though but sometimes I can just look at my husband and he knows what I have seen or am thinking immediately. He always laughs! My other somewhat zany tendency is to make up alternative song lyrics to a tune I like, that say all sorts of random things relevant to whatever I am thinking at that moment. They are rubbish mostly but usually scan and rhyme well to the tune, and when they don't, I make them more out of time as part of the fun. The contents can be crazy. I cannot give you any examples because I never remember them. I also love to sing and sometimes when my husband is playing guitar I can sing along and stay in tune but that doesn't matter.

Why am I telling you all this? Well I want you to find and enjoy your own extraordinary zany qualities too. I think this approach to life, which is playful and fun, is the antidote to the burdens of responsibility we have adopted as a species in our desire for security and other such nebulous paradigms.

I believe that being zany or extraordinary is what lifts humanity out of the doldrums and enhances creativity, openness, laughter and love far more than all the heavy burdens of life. Yes of course we all need to be responsible as I wrote about in its own chapter, but beyond that we should also live lightly. So I have my bouncing expressions, and my grandson is already showing a strong propensity for similar expressions of joy with life. And that makes me happy indeed. But bouncing might not be for you. Find your own equivalents though and express it for all you are worth. Find your joy and let it free.

Don't worry about how others see you; take it all in your stride because if you have read this far you know how to do that pretty well by now. And then you are more likely to reach the zenith of your life, your highest point of happiness. Just make sure that your happiness is intrinsic to you and never dependent on external factors, never open to being bought and sold, never vulnerable to destruction by casual unkindness.

Zany, eccentric, difficult, an individual, great or a burden, whichever it is that I am, it is all I can be and all I will ever be. It doesn't matter, it is how I am and I know I am loved, and I love deeply.

Does it matter how any of us are, as long as we do not go around being unkind to others or hurting them in ignorance.

Embrace your diversity, love life, enjoy the journey.

Last Words

Thank you for reading and for sharing my journey with me. I can't think of much more to share with you on this journey through the alphabet, though there are lots more ideas and chapters for inclusion in the other parts of this series. I hope you have found it useful and possibly inspirational for your own journeys.

There is only ever one person we can help and that is our self. This is the most important work we can ever do. E can only help others by example and allow them to make the changes in their own time. It took me a long time to understand this fully, but it took me a long time to learn my own lessons and to unpick all the old paradigms. We can all help each other. This is what will make the world a better place for everyone to live in. That is my greatest hope. Thank you for reading. Xxx

If you wish to disagree with, or to further explore anything I have written here please feel free to contact me via Medium.com where I post my thought pieces regularly or on my email at sylvia.clare@btinternet.com

Travelling the Alphabet Emotionally

Books and Topics to come - all are in process of being written as the muse takes me, which one makes it past the finishing post next is anybody's guess.

Travelling the Alphabet Spiritually

Travelling the Alphabet Geographically

Travelling the Alphabet – Random Destinations

Gee Mum - Thanks for the Challenges

Dharma Talk

My second book of poetry – In What Do I Take Refuge?

32449026R00162

Printed in Poland
by Amazon Fulfillment
Poland Sp. z o.o., Wrocław